Just Fix It

Tom Feiza
Mr. Fix-It

Published by **Mr. Fix-It Press**

Published by:
Mr. Fix-It Press
4620 South Raven Lane
New Berlin, WI 53151
phone: (262) 786-7878
fax: (262) 786-7877
email: Tom@misterfix-it.com

NOTICE:
This book is available at special discounts for bulk purchases, sales promotions, premiums, fund raising, or educational use. For details, write, phone, fax or email the publisher.

First Edition

ISBN # 0-9674759-0-2

Library of Congress Catalog Card # 99-96033

Printed in the United States of America

DEDICATION

Who made me Mr. Fix-It?

I owe a lot to Uncle Nick and Uncle Joe in Virgil, Illinois, who put me on the road to being a real fix-it guy. I worked at their dairy farms, racetrack and motorcycle shop and on their many construction projects.

I was nine years old when Uncle Nick began paying me 50 cents a day to work on his farm. When I graduated from Marquette University Engineering School, I was still working for and learning from Nick and Joe and their crews.

They taught me that you learn by doing. From Uncle Nick and Uncle Joe, I learned the value of hard and honest effort.

My mom was also a great fix-it lady who taught me a lot about painting and refinishing. We still share information today.

What is my house like?

Ask Gayle, my wife and best friend. She will tell you we have a lot of fix-it projects waiting for me. Just like every other couple, we operate with a "honey-do" list—you know, "Honey, you need to do this." And when the list gets too long, we talk about hiring a contractor. Our home is just like every other home.

So this book is dedicated to . . .

My wife, Gayle, and my kids, Lindsay and Tom III, for putting up with all my fix-it projects and my basement full of stuff; and to my mom, Uncle Nick, and Uncle Joe.

ACKNOWLEDGMENTS

Special thanks go to all the people who listen to my radio show, watch my television appearances, attend my seminars, and read my newspaper column. Your questions and tips made this book possible.

Many tool and product manufactures have provided me with excellent technical information and products to test and use.

My editor, Leah Carson, took my rough copy and made the information much more useful and user-friendly. Jack Pachuta patiently encouraged me and walked me through the publishing and printing process. Lynn Eckstein designed my Mr. Fix-It logo years ago, and her great cover design really got me excited about this book.

Artwork came from product manufacturers and from John Krigger and Alan Carson. See the back of this book for more on John and Alan's excellent information about homes.

Most importantly, I owe a lot to my wife, Gayle, and our kids, Lindsay and Tom. They helped me keep things in proper perspective by dragging me out of the basement and off the ladder for vacations and family time.

Please enjoy my book and have a great Fix-It day!

TABLE OF CONTENTS

INTRODUCTION 1

PAINTING 3

Surface preparation 3

Paint selection 5

Mess protection 6

Caulk joints for a professional finish 7

Tools take the pain out of painting 7

Paint the ceiling first?...or the walls? 8

Brushing up on paintbrush basics 8

Painting over textured surfaces 9

Cleanup after the job 10

All spackling compounds are not created equal! 10

POP go the nails in drywall 11

Wall-Art: painting over crayon and marker 11

Conquering stain bleed-through 11

When paint peels from bathroom walls 12

Painting mildewed areas 12

Remove dried paint splatters easily 14

Repainting kitchen cabinets 14

Painting your fiberboard garage door 15

Painting rain gutters and metal railings 15

Restoring (painting) sandstone on a fireplace 16

The easy way to paint dark paneling 17

Staining a steel door 18

WALLPAPERING   19

Removing old wallpaper   19

Wallpaper seam repair   20

Wallpaper secret—the primer   20

WOOD FINISHING AND REPAIR   21

Preventing bubbles and "craters" in varnish   21

Wood filler and putty: the finishing touch to woodworking projects   21

Refinishing kitchen cabinets   22

Fixing scratches in stained woodwork   23

Refinishing wood furniture   26

Use stripper pads, not steel wool   27

Stripping paint from wood pores   27

Refinishing a damaged front door   27

Removing stains from an oak floor   28

Safe finishes for children's wooden toys   30

No need to oil or "feed" wood finishes   30

CLEANING AND STAIN REMOVAL   33

My secret weapon for stain removal   33

The secret Mr. Fix-It window washing formula   34

Cleaning glass doors on a fireplace   34

Keeping a shower clean   34

Cleaning the bathtub and shower   36

Removing hard water stains from a glass shower door   37

Grout—keeping it clean   38

Removing hair spray buildup from bathroom surfaces   38

Cleaning old porcelain bathroom fixtures 39

Cleaning white film from coffeemaker 39

Banish stains around cabinet door handles 40

Restoring Formica countertops 40

Removing Super Glue from a countertop 41

Removing marker stains from paint and woodwork 41

Removing a white ring from a wooden coffee table 42

Removing stains from marble 42

Removing masking tape 43

Removing old shelf paper 43

Cleaning and polishing brass-colored metal 44

Cleaning a stone fireplace 44

HEATING AND AIR CONDITIONING **47**

Understanding your forced-air furnace 47

High-efficiency gas furnaces feel cooler 48

When a high-efficiency furnace stops producing heat 49

Heating and cooling adjustments—forced air furnace 49

Furnace air filters and maintenance 51

Service requirements for older furnaces 53

Noises from the heating/cooling system 54

Use your windows to help your air conditioner 55

Central air conditioner, part 1: to cover or
  not to cover? 55

Central air conditioner, part 2: seasonal shutdown
  and re-starting 56

What does a "ton" of air conditioning mean? 57

Rerouting a hose that drains your heating/cooling system   58

Reducing severe dampness throughout the house   59

Reducing basement dampness in the summer   60

Heating a basement recreation room   61

Excessive winter dryness indoors   62

APPLIANCES   65

Clean those refrigerator coils   65

When moving a refrigerator, wait a while before restarting   66

Repairing balky gas stovetop burners   66

Touch-ups make appliances look like new   67

Painting metal finishes of interior furnishings   67

Rust on dishwasher racks? Act now!   67

LIGHTING   69

When a fluorescent light buzzes   69

Burning odor from light fixture or outlet   69

Removing broken light bulbs   70

Energy-saving tips for light bulbs   71

ELECTRICAL   73

Installing and maintaining a GFCI (ground fault circuit interrupter)   73

Doorbell blues   74

PLUMBING, SINKS, TUBS   77

Repair a dripping faucet   77

Dripping valves—interior   78

Dripping garden hoses   78

Dripping water heater   79

Garbage disposal tips and repair   79

Leaking sink mushroom (air gap)   81

Leaking toilet tank – So your toilet fills
        during the night?   82

Re-caulking around the bathtub   83

Preventing grout stains   84

Clean a plugged shower head   85

Low flow at the faucet or washing machine   85

Toilet trouble #1: partial flush   85

Toilet trouble #2: blockage   87

Toilet trouble #3: whistling sounds   87

Banging pipes (water hammer)   88

Preventing water pipe freeze-ups   90

Coping with a popping water heater   91

Pilot light on a gas water heater   93

Sump pump clunking   93

WALLS, CEILINGS, WINDOWS AND DOORS   **95**

Adjusting a sliding patio screen door that sticks   95

Replacing the screen in a screen door   96

Adjusting sliding closet doors that stick   97

Finding parts for old double-hung windows   98

"Popped" drywall nails   98

Secret drywall finishing method   99

Patching cracks in the ceiling   99

BASEMENT, FOUNDATION   **101**

Bailing out basement window wells   101

Sump pump basics   102

When roots invade your sump pump crock...   104

Sealing a concrete basement floor   105

ODORS   **107**

Musty smell from sink   107

Smelly garbage disposal   107

Sewer smell in home   107

Sewer smell from toilet   109

Water supply smells like rotten eggs   109

Burning odor from light fixture   110

Eliminating refrigerator odor   111

Eliminating musty smells from wood furnishings   112

Removing smoke smells from home or car   112

Pet urine odors   113

SAFETY MEASURES   **115**

In case of emergency: things everyone in the
  household should know   115

Ensuring safe venting of a clothes dryer   119

Carbon monoxide detectors   119

Radon testing in your home   120

Asbestos in your home—what to do   121

Securing slippery throw rugs   122

MYSTERIES, MISERIES   **123**

Restoring Formica countertops   123

Gray vinyl-flooring stains around a toilet   123

Quieting a squeaky floor   124

Opening the garage door during a power outage   126

Mildewed walls or ceilings   126

EXTERIOR MAINTENANCE   **129**

Sealing pressure-treated wood   129

Sealing a cedar deck   130

Cleaning the cracks between deck boards   131

Patching rotted wood   131

Cleaning and/or repainting metal siding   132

Removing stains from vinyl siding   134

Discouraging woodpeckers from pecking
    cedar siding   135

Renew rusty wrought iron railings   135

When exterior varnish peels...   136

Broken chimney cap   136

Quick patch for rain gutters   137

Tightening loose rain gutters   138

Why roof shingles get black streaks   138

Cleaning dirt and stains from a concrete driveway   139

Sealing concrete   143

Sealing the gap between driveway and garage   143

Repairing broken concrete surfaces   144

Mudjacking to level exterior concrete   146

RECOMMENDED HOME REPAIR MANUALS   **149**

IMPORTANT CONTACTS   **151**

INDEX   **171**

ABOUT THE AUTHOR

Tom Feiza, Mr. Fix-It, is a recovering mechanical engineer and a real life fix-it guy.

Tom worked on a farm through grade school, high school and college. After graduating from Marquette University as a mechanical engineer, Tom worked for over 20 years in the construction, maintenance and operation of large facilities. Then he shifted from engineering to become Mr. Fix-It, helping people with their home maintenance and repair problems.

Tom now combines his hobby, his passion and his profession into his unique enterprise—Tom Feiza, Mr. Fix-It, Inc.

Tom hosts a live radio call-in show on AM 620 WTMJ in Milwaukee, Wisconsin. More than 50 newspapers carry his question-and-answer column, and he often appears on television, providing home repair tips.

Tom presents unique and entertaining how-to seminars at home shows and retail events. He also gives entertaining keynotes at dinner meetings and professional conventions.

In another venture that helps him stay in touch with homes and their problems, Tom provides home inspection services and engineering advice for residential construction.

INTRODUCTION

BE SAFE!

The information in this book has been carefully assembled to ensure that it is as accurate as possible. However, the book provides general information only, and it is sold with the understanding that the publisher and author are not rendering legal or professional services.

When attempting a home repair project, always consult professionals and always follow label directions. Companies that manufacture home repair products are the ultimate authorities. Follow their instructions.

Many home repair projects involve a certain degree of risk and should be approached with care. You should only attempt repairs if you have read and understood the instructions for the product or tool you are using. If questions or problems arise, consult a professional or the manufacturer.

Due to the variability of local conditions, construction materials, and personal skills, neither the author nor the publisher assumes responsibility for any injuries suffered or for damages or other losses that may result from the information presented.

Chapter 1

PAINTING

Surface preparation
Surface preparation is the most important step in a successful painting project. Before painting, evaluate the surface. It should be smooth, clean and non-glossy.

Cleaning
A dirty or greasy surface must be cleaned, or paint will not bond well. Wash from the bottom up to avoid runs and streaks. Use an easy-to-rinse cleanser, because if there's detergent residue left on the wall, new paint may not bond. I like Spic & Span, Soilax, and Mex. Mex is the strongest - it will even remove some paint and shellac -so use it carefully. Ammonia and water, mixed in proportions recommended on the label, also makes a good cleanser that doesn't leave residue.

Shiny surfaces can be dulled with sandpaper, steel wool, or 3M Synthetic Steel Wool pads. Mex often removes gloss as it cleans. You can also use de-glossing chemicals, but they are strong solvents and you need to take safety precautions.

If there is mildew on the walls, you must remove it with a stronger cleaner: mix two cups of laundry bleach per gallon of cleaner. Don't ever mix bleach with ammonia or ammonia cleaners.

Smooth the surface
Spackling compound, joint compound, scrapers, and sandpaper or sanding screens are the tools for smoothing. Remove all loose paint by scraping and sanding. Fill gaps with spackling compound or joint compound. Always use joint compound for larger gaps and large flat areas, because it's much easier to smooth onto the surface.

When sanding large areas, use a large sanding pad mounted on a pole. Consider using sanding screens rather than sandpaper. The screens don't plug, and the pole allows you to use your whole body in the sanding motion.

Repair problem cracks
If cracks reappear after patching, use Krack-Kote to fill them. It remains flexible and will not re-crack.

Painter's caulk works well for joints and gaps, and for small cracks that reoccur. Caulk is a great filler for wall-to-ceiling or corner joints. Also, use caulk to fill around moldings or trim that you will be painting.

Wider cracks require tape reinforcement and a wide patch to blend into the surrounding surface. Invest in wide-bladed tools for a professional finish.

Priming
New, bare surfaces should always be primed to provide a smooth, nonporous base. If the surface has stains from water, crayon, or markers, these can be covered with Bin, Kilz, or similar primers. You must prime stains like these to keep them from bleeding through latex paint. I like Bin. It is quick-

PAINTING

drying and low-odor. It is shellac-based, so you can clean up tools afterward with ammonia and water.

Paint selection
When it comes to paint, quality is in direct proportion to cost. You get what you pay for. Cheap paint has fewer ingredients, less expensive ingredients, and more water or solvent. Quality paints cover better, are easier to apply, and spatter less. Paint is a small part of the cost of the job, so buy the best.

Interior
Gloss or semi-gloss paints are usually recommended for kitchens, bathrooms, and high-traffic areas where the surfaces may need cleaning. But remember that a glossy surface shows all the imperfections, while flat finishes are great at hiding imperfections. Most modern decorators choose flat paints because of their appearance and ability to hide imperfections.

For woodwork and trim, oil-based paints are much more durable. They dry to a harder finish. Once dry, they resist scratches and are easier to wash. Today's oil paints are low-odor and easy to apply and they also cover well.

Exterior—test for type of paint
If you moved into an existing home with a painted exterior, sooner or later you'll need to repaint. Maybe you're wondering what kind of paint was used, or you simply want to know which type of paint is best.

To find out what type of paint is on the surface now, clean a small area with detergent to remove dirt and paint dust. Then dampen a rag with ammonia or denatured alcohol and rub the surface. If paint comes off on the rag, you have a latex paint.

The gloss of the finish does not reveal whether it is latex or oil-based. However, oil-based paints tend to cure harder and maintain a higher gloss. An oil-based paint is your best choice when the surface shows heavy "chalking"—powder that comes off on your hand when you rub the paint. Oil-based paint (or primer) will bond better than latex to chalky surfaces.

Oil-based paint is also your best choice when painting a surface that has four or more layers of old oil-based paint. To determine the number of existing paint coats, try cutting through layers of the paint or removing a chip. Layers of paint will be evident in a cross section of the surface.

Modern oil-based paints are much easier to use than the "old" oil paints. But you do need to clean up your tools and any spatters with solvent. Oil paints also have more odor, but they are silky smooth and easy to apply.

Mess protection

When painting indoors, clear the space and mask off woodwork, trim and fixtures. Don't settle for cheap masking tape; it won't work well. Painter-quality masking tape like KleenEdge and 3M Long Mask have a special adhesive that bonds tightly to the surface you're protecting.

My favorite masking product is Easy Mask Painting Tape. This is a masking paper with sticky adhesive on one edge. The adhesive bonds well to all smooth surfaces and can be removed easily. After applying this masking paper to base molding, you can raise it slightly to slide your drop cloth underneath. Easy Mask is wide enough to cover base moldings and most wood trim. For about $3, you can mask several typical rooms. I use the 4-inch-wide Easy Mask at the base molding and fold up the edge to lap over my dropcloth.

Quick Mask and similar 8- to 21-inch-wide masking products with a poly or paper dropcloth attached are also very effective. The key to applying any masking product is to first clean or dust the surface, because tape will not stick to dirt. As you apply the tape, rub the leading edge with a knife or fingernail to fasten it securely.

Caulk joints for a professional finish
To create a smooth-looking finish, professional painters often caulk interior joints around moldings and trim. You can use inexpensive acrylic "painter's caulk" to fill gaps and voids, creating a smooth, crisp paint line over the caulk. This painter's caulk is designed to be painted soon after it is applied.

Tools take the pain out of painting
The right tools can make interior painting quick and easy—so toss that roller tray, and forget the ladder. Flimsy paint trays tip, don't hold enough paint and are hard to clean. Moving or climbing a ladder with the paint tray is precarious at best.

Instead, you need:

- a 5-gallon plastic pail
- a roller screen
- an ordinary paint roller
- an extension pole

You can often get a 5-gallon pail free from contractors or at construction sites. Add a roller screen - a small piece of heavy metal screen that hangs inside the pail. These are available at larger paint dealers.

When you use the 5-gallon pail, you can intermix several gallons of paint, which is required for custom-blended paint. A 5-gallon pail also cuts down on refill time (unlike using a tray, when you're making frequent trips to refill it from the can). The pail prevents spills, and it's easy to clean when you're done.

The extension pole eliminates the need for a ladder. Buy an adjustable pole. It costs a few dollars more, but that's worth it for a pole that lets you easily reach varying heights. Attach the pole to the roller. Keep the 5-gallon pail on the floor. Dip the roller into the paint, then roll it over the screen to even out the amount of paint.

The pole will allow you to fill the roller and paint high and low on the walls without bending or stretching. You can even paint ceilings while standing on the floor.

Working from the floor is safer, and it lets you use your legs, shoulders, and full upper body while painting.
One word of caution: Don't be tempted to roll too quickly. The pole allows you to shift into high gear, but paint can really splatter.

Paint the ceiling first? . . . or the walls?
Paint the ceiling first to simplify cutting in at the ceiling-to-wall joint. When painting the ceiling, you can lap paint onto the wall. Later, cutting in from the wall to the ceiling is easy, because paint does not flow up. You'll probably be touching up this area with a brush, and from that angle you can see what you're doing.

Brushing up on paintbrush basics
When the area you're painting is too small or irregular for a roller, obviously you'll use a brush instead. Matching a paintbrush to the paint you're using is essential for good results.

PAINTING

There are three basic types of paintbrushes to consider.

Natural bristle brushes are used only with alkyd or oil-based paints and finishes. Bristles are made with animal hair. Natural brushes give the smooth surface desirable with gloss finishes. However, if used with water-based paint, natural bristle brushes will absorb water, become limp, and fail to hold paint.

Synthetic bristle brushes are required for water-based (latex) paint products. They are made from nylon, polyester or similar fiber. A good quality synthetic brush can also be used with oil-based paint.

 Foam brushes are inexpensive and are handy for any quick, small painting chore. They can't provide the quality application and control of a bristle brush, but they are so inexpensive they can be discarded after use to avoid cleanup.

By the way, it isn't always necessary to clean your brush when you take a break from painting. You can wrap your brush tightly in aluminum foil or plastic wrap for up to one hour without a problem. For a longer break, place the wrapped brush in the freezer. When you're ready to use it again, thaw it out. To temporarily store a roller with paint on it, use a tube container like the ones Pringles potato chips are sold in.

Painting over textured surfaces
Most homes have a light sand finish on walls and ceilings. Matching this texture can be a real challenge. Lightweight-textured sand often turns into lumpy "lead shot" when mixed with paint. I've had good luck, though, with pre-mixed textured

paint. I water it down and apply it with a standard roller or brush. Play with the thickness and application technique until you have a match. USG-1 is a good textured paint product.

Cleanup after the job

If you've invested $15 or $20 in a quality paintbrush, you'll want to maintain it well. Use water and detergent to clean latex paint; use paint thinner for oil paints. Always clean a brush immediately after use. Never let it stand on its bristles in the bottom of the paint can.

Use a brush comb to remove paint from between the bristles and to straighten the bristle as you clean the brush. Use  the comb one last time after the bristles are clean. Wrap the clean brush in its original container or in clean paper, and hang it up to dry. The wrapper keeps the bristles in shape.

For rollers, consider buying a spinner to remove paint residue. Also, a roller cleaner—a plastic donut for a water hose—works well to rinse rollers clean.

But the greatest roller cleaner is a Roller-Saver, which cleans and dries a roller in 30 seconds. The Roller-Saver's small plastic chamber has internal water jets. You attach this chamber to a water source and place the roller cover inside the tube. Water is forced through the roller, spinning it clean. Turn off the water quickly, and the roller spins dry.

All spackling compounds are not created equal!

Try one of the new lightweight spackling compounds the next time you do minor repairs on drywall. These don't shrink, and small patches can be painted over within a few minutes. For small areas like nail holes, apply the compound with your finger—it's easy to match the texture on most walls or ceilings.

PAINTING

Older vinyl spackling compounds are okay, but these are softer and runny. They require several coats because they shrink. You can easily identify the lightweight compounds by the lightness of the filled container compared to vinyl compounds.

POP go the nails in drywall

Occasionally, nails pop out of drywall as a home's wood framing swells or shrinks with seasonal changes in temperature and humidity. To repair the pop, either pull the offending nail or drive it below the surface. Then secure the drywall with two drywall screws set a few inches away from the problem nail. The screws will hold much tighter than the original nail. Finally, spackle the area, prime and repaint.

Wall-Art: painting over crayon and marker

Have the young artists in your family drawn on the walls with crayons or markers? You'll want to repaint without letting the stain bleed through.

First, wash the wall with strong detergent to remove most of the wax and stain. Then seal the damaged areas with a shellac or oil-based primer/stain killer such as Bin or Kilz. This sealer will cover the stain, prevent bleed-through, and provide a good base for the final coat of paint.

Conquering stain bleed-through

The procedure described above will also help if dark stains of any type are bleeding through a finish coat of paint. Apply a sealer such as Bin or Kilz. Most paint manufacturers have their own brands, too. These are oil or shellac-based with a white pigment. Some are sold in spray cans to cover small areas. They dry quickly and can be painted over in just a few hours.

When paint peels from bathroom walls

Older homes with no exhaust fan in the bathroom often have paint problems. The paint peels, develops mildew, and just looks bad. Opening a door or window may help with ventilation, but excessive moisture, mildew, and peeling paint remain. What can you do?

The best solution is to have an exhaust fan installed. Perhaps you can mount a fan in an exterior wall or route the exhaust line through the basement.

To reduce moisture in the bathroom after a shower, wipe down wet surfaces, remove wet towels, and keep the bathroom door open. Consider using a small fan to circulate air into the hall.

You can also apply a special paint that resists mildew and peeling. First, kill existing mildew with laundry bleach and water. Use 2 cups of bleach in a gallon of detergent water. Scrape away any loose paint, and sand the surfaces smooth. Spackle as needed.

Then paint with Zinsser brand Perma-White Bathroom Wall and Ceiling Paint. It's a self-priming paint, so you should apply two coats. This white satin or semi-gloss paint can be tinted. I have used this paint for several years with great success. It is guaranteed to resist mildew and peeling.

Painting mildewed areas
Interior
For mildewed walls or ceilings, proper painting requires killing mildew first, then using special paint. You can kill mildew with a strong detergent solution and laundry bleach. Add about 2 to 4 cups of bleach per gallon of detergent water. Read the label of the detergent carefully to make sure it's safe to mix bleach with your detergent.

PAINTING

After allowing the surface to dry, apply Bin primer to stained areas. Then paint with two coats of Zinsser brand Perma-White Bathroom Wall and Ceiling Paint.

Exterior
Some homes develop mildew on eaves or overhangs, especially if they're in a shady area that's not well ventilated. The solution is to clean the surfaces, kill the mildew and repaint. This assumes the wood is still in good condition.

If the wood is rotted or swollen, you need to replace it or cover it with siding. For painting, wash the area with a commercial mildewcide. A good paint store will help you select cleaning and painting materials.

I have had great success using Jomax for cleaning and mildew removal. Mix a small amount of Jomax with laundry bleach and water. Spray the solution on the area with a garden sprayer and wait about 15 minutes. Rinse well.

For heavy stains, scrub with a soft brush and rinse well. I like to use a brush attached to a long handle. I can reach farther and use my back and legs for the scrubbing.

You can also clean with a strong detergent like a TSP substitute and a few cups of laundry bleach per gallon of water. Whatever cleaner or chemical you use, follow all the label safety precautions and protect plant materials in the area by spraying the plants with water and covering them with plastic.

After the area is clean and the bleach or commercial cleaner has killed the mildew, allow the wood to dry for several days. Paint with a mildew-resistant paint or add mildewcide to the paint. Zinsser makes a great mildew-resistant exterior paint.

To prevent mildew from returning, improve the air circulation by trimming branches in mildew-prone areas. Routine washing with a product like Jomax will keep the surfaces clean and discourage mildew, which feeds on dirt.

Remove dried paint splatters easily

Several products on the market remove dried latex paint splatters without harming stained or varnished wood. Try Goof Off, Oops, or a similar solvent, available at paint and hardware stores.

Saturate a cloth with the solvent. Dampen the splatter, then rub lightly to remove the paint. (Test an inconspicuous area first.) Be careful, since these products are flammable and may also remove softened varnish.

Repainting kitchen cabinets

You can successfully paint stained and varnished kitchen cabinets. The biggest challenge is providing a good surface for the new gloss paint. Surface imperfections will show through the paint, and an improperly prepared surface can prevent the paint from adhering properly.

Start by removing all doors and hardware. Use a power pad sander and medium grit sandpaper to sand the surfaces. Where the varnish has softened, you may need to use a solvent refinisher or stripper instead, because soft varnish can clog sandpaper.

Vacuum up all dust. Wash the surfaces with a liquid solvent deglosser, then rub your hand over the surfaces. Any imperfections you can feel and see will show through the paint. Continue sanding to remove these imperfections. When the surfaces are as smooth as possible, clean once more, then prime with an oil or shellac-based stain killer/primer such as Bin.

PAINTING

Buy the best oil-based paint available and follow the manufacturer's instructions. Often two coats are required. Use a natural bristle brush. Lay the doors flat for painting.

Let the surfaces dry for several days and provide plenty of
ventilation. Then carefully assemble the doors and hardware.

Painting your fiberboard garage door

A properly painted garage door will last for many, many years.
I see many newer garage doors with fiberboard panels that
have turned to mush because they were not painted properly.

First, wash the door with a strong detergent and a scrub
brush, and then rinse thoroughly.

Prime the door with a water-based stain killer or an oil-based
primer. Finish with a high quality acrylic exterior house paint
or trim paint.

Remember to paint all six sides of each door panel—outside,
inside, lower edge, top edge, and two sides. If you neglect
any side, water stains will develop. You will need to raise and
lower the door to paint on the sides that close around the
hinges. Many people miss the edges and this causes the door
to fail prematurely.

Painting rain gutters and metal railings

For rusty metal on rain gutters, flashings, or metal railings, try
one of the rust converter products. They provide a tannin and
a organic polymer. Tannin converts rust to a stable blue-black
compound. Organic polymer provides a protective layer. Rust
Reformer from Rustoleum and Extend Rust Treatment from
Loctite are two common brands.

Scrape away the loose rust with a wire brush, but you don't
need to reach bare metal. (This "saves" the metal on thin gut-

ters and flashing.) Apply the milky rust converter with a brush. The rusty area will turn blue-black. The reaction should be cured after 24 hours.

The converter works like a primer. You can then apply a top coat of exterior paint. Some of these products allow you to apply two coats, using the product itself as a finish coat. Don't sand the converted metal or you will lose the protection. Follow specific instructions for the product you are using.

Restoring (painting) sandstone on a fireplace

If sandstone around a fireplace becomes stained or dirty, painting can restore it. First, scrub the surface with a strong detergent such as Soilax or TSP substitute. Rinse well. Then prime the stone with Bulls Eye 1-2-3 or an oil-based primer. You may need to use several primer coats to create a smoother finish, because the stone will soak up paint.

Finally, paint with the finish of your choice. Again, you may need to use several coats. When choosing a paint color, remember that painted surfaces exposed to heat may discolor. Instead of painting, consider seeking the advice of a company that designs and installs fireplaces. They may have an effective alternative, such as facing with a new stone veneer. They could also cover the hearth with a tile and provide a wood mantle.

If the mantle also needs updating, you can have any good carpenter or millwork shop make a fireplace mantle. A finish carpenter can make a beautiful mantle using standard wood trim parts. Larger lumberyards and millwork shops often have mantles on display and will custom build them for your specific needs.

Most fireplace stores have great showrooms with fireplaces

PAINTING

you can see and touch. This is a great way to get ideas and help with decisions on re-working your fireplace.

The easy way to paint dark paneling

The 1970s brought us family rooms finished with dark, dark paneling. You can brighten up your paneling with proper preparation and a coat of light paint. Light walls will lighten up the room, making it feel larger. Painting avoids the mess of removing the paneling, damaging the drywall and reworking all the wood trim.

Start by washing the paneling with strong detergent like Soilax, TSP, or Spic and Span. This removes accumulated grime and slightly roughens the glossy surface. If shiny smooth areas still exist, scrub them with a deglosser solvent or lightly sand the paneling.

Deglosser solvent is available at any paint store. You must clean and roughen shiny areas so a new finish will stick. While washing paneling, re-nail any loose areas you find.

Priming is a vital step. Prime with a stain killer/primer such as Bin or Kilz. These products are specially formulated to cover stains and problem materials. They also provide a white base for the finish coat.

Finally, paint the paneling with a finish coat of 100% acrylic latex paint. Buy a top-quality paint. Two coats may be required. The highest quality paints have 100% acrylic binders. Also, acrylic paint is durable and easy to apply, and it cleans up with soap and water.

That's all it takes to have a family room that looks lighter and brighter. The texture and grooves in most types of paneling also add character to the walls.

Staining a steel door

You can create a wood-grain look on a door made of steel or fiberglass by using a thick-bodied stain and a graining tool.

Zar's stain and texturing tool is appropriate for this job. Apply the stain, then draw the tool across it, creating the appearance of textured grain. If you're not satisfied with the results, you can wipe off the stain and start over. Creating a realistic grain will take a little practice.

When you are satisfied with the results, allow the stain to dry. Then apply a thin coat of stain to the whole door, giving the entire surface a wood color. When that coat dries, finish with a coat of Zar Exterior Polyurethane in the direction of the grain.

I suggest you use compatible products and tools throughout the job. Zar makes products specifically designed to finish steel doors with a wood grain, and also provides more detailed instructions.

Chapter 2

WALLPAPERING

Removing old wallpaper

Removing wallpaper can be tough or tougher. It is never easy. The trick is to find someone experienced to help you.

To see what type of paper you have, peel up a corner. If the wall covering tears and the surface is the texture of rough paper, you have paper type wall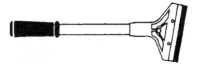
covering. This type must removed with steam or a remover chemical applied directly to the paper surface. After the paper is loose, scrape with a sharp, stiff wall paper scraper.

If the wall covering surface is shiny and smooth but still tears when you lift a corner, you have a vinyl-coated paper. It needs to be scored with rough sandpaper so steam or remover chemical can penetrate the surface. You can also puncture the surface with a special tool called a "Paper Tiger" made by Zinsser Company.

If the wall covering surface pulls up in large chunks, you have solid vinyl paper. With this type, you pull away the vinyl covering and the paper backing stays stuck on the wall. The paper backing is removed with steam or a chemical.

For large jobs, consider renting a wallpaper steamer. If the wall has several coats of paper, a steamer is in order.

For single coats of paper, enzyme removers like DIF Wallpaper Stripper or DIF Gel work well. These strippers have a penetrating agent that helps water penetrate the surface and an enzyme that breaks down the adhesive. You apply several coats over about 30 minutes and let the chemical do the work. Once loose, the paper must be scraped or pulled from the wall.

Wash the wall with remover chemical to remove adhesive residue. Allow the wall to dry well. If you plan to paint the surface, prime it first.

Wallpaper seam repair
Special adhesive for closing wallpaper seams is available at most wallpaper and hardware stores. Apply the adhesive to the wallpaper at the seam and lay it back in place. "Stick-Ease" is an excellent product.

Wallpaper secret - the primer
The secret to a fun wallpaper application job is properly priming the surface. Primer simplifies hanging the paper and aids in its eventual removal.

A primed surface allows you to slide the paper into position before it is "welded" in place by the adhesive. When a wall is not primed, adhesive dries quickly as moisture is drawn into the wall surface. The paper can't be positioned and the adhesive can fail. Failed adhesive causes the seams to open up, and the paper may be on the floor in the morning.

Primer also seals the surface so the paper can be removed easily with water and a remover chemical.

Primer is specifically designed for wall coverings and is applied like paint. Zinsser and Golden Harvest both make a great water-based primer.

Chapter 3

WOOD FINISH-ING AND REPAIR

Preventing bubbles and "craters" in varnish

If not properly applied, wood varnish can develop bubbles that remain on the surface or pop to form craters. To prevent bubbling, never shake a container of varnish—stir it *gently*.

Bubbles also appear during rapid application with a foam brush. Another cause of bubbles: tapping the brush on the container to remove the excess after dipping in the varnish. If there's too much varnish on the brush, gently press the brush against the side of the container.

Wood filler and putty: the finishing touch to woodworking projects

For a perfect finish to varnished woodwork or other woodworking projects, fill all nail holes and voids. Voids disappear when filled flush to the surface with properly colored putty. Stain the wood first, then fill the holes with putty after the stain has dried. This enables you to perfectly match the color without depending on the stain to color the filler.

The quickest and least expensive way to obtain putty of the correct color is to mix your own. Buy small containers of putty in light oak and dark walnut colors. Blend small portions of each color until it's the right shade. In some cases you'll also need to blend in some red mahogany color.

Once you have spent several dollars on two or three basic colors, you can custom-mix a wide variety of shades. With oil-based putty in resealable containers, you'll be set for years. Any custom-mixed putty left over can be stored with the original color putty without problem.

Refinishing kitchen cabinets
Painted surface
If the old surface was painted, you must remove the paint with a chemical stripper. For more information, see "Repainting kitchen cabinets" in the "Painting" chapter.

Stained/varnished surface
If the old surface was stained and/or varnished, you can refinish the cabinets just as fine furniture is refinished. You can either remove most of the varnish/stain with a chemical refinisher, or you can just clean the surface well.

In any case, first take the doors off the cabinets and remove handles and other hardware. This will make the project easier, and the results will look more professional. Lay the doors flat when you work on them.

If the only damage to the finish is dark stains around the door handles, you can simply clean these areas. Try using 3M synthetic steel wool pads instead of real steel wool. The pads hold together very well. They won't poke your fingers or catch on the wood grain.

Scrub the stains with a pad dipped in mineral spirits, turpentine, or paint thinner. Then lightly scrub the whole surface, cleaning and dulling it so the new finish will stick.

Follow safety precautions. Wear protective clothing and make sure the work area has good ventilation. All of these products are flammable; some are extremely flammable. Follow any

WOOD FINISHING AND REPAIR

other safety precautions on the label. Some refinisher chemicals contain methylene chloride and may cause blindness. After the surface is clean and the dark stains are removed, apply a clear wipe-on oil finish as described below under "Clean finish."

If you need to redo more than just a few stained areas, chemical refinishing is necessary. A refinisher is a strong solvent cleaner that dissolves and removes part of the old varnish. When choosing which refinisher to use, visit a quality paint store or paint department where you can get good advice. Many companies offer refinishers like those made popular by Homer Formby.

As chemical refinisher removes the finish, it also evens out the color of the wood and stain. You work in a small area, scrubbing the finish with steel wool or a 3M synthetic steel wool pad. As the steel wool becomes clogged with dirty finish, you rinse the pad in more refinisher.

Once you've scrubbed the whole surface, it will be smooth and evenly colored. If not, wipe down the whole piece with clean refinisher and clean steel wool in long, overlapping strokes. Most of the stain color will remain, and the wood will be very smooth.

Clear finish
After cleaning or refinishing, apply an oil-based wipe-on clear finish such as Minwax Antique Oil Finish, tung oil, or General Finishes Royal Finish (my favorite). All are low-odor and can be applied with a rag. Most are available in either glossy or satin finish. Using several coats will produce a thicker finish.

Fixing scratches in stained woodwork
"Quick and simple" rarely describes repairs to wood finishes. But you can try these tricks.

When scratches appear lighter than the surrounding dark-stained woodwork, it usually means either that the scratch goes through the stain into the wood or that the varnish is flaking off.

Restoring the clear finish
Inspect the scratches carefully. If you can see flaking varnish with dark-stained wood underneath, you just need to restore the clear finish. Rub the loose varnish with fine steel wool or fine synthetic steel wool until you have removed the flaking varnish and slightly roughened a small area of the finish surrounding the scratch.

With the tip of rag, a small brush, or even a cotton swab, apply a thin coat of a wipe-on oil finish like General Finishes Royal Finish or UGL Wipe On Tung Oil. These finishes work well because they will bond to the existing finish. Apply finish to the damaged area only. You may need several coats to hide the scratch.

Re-staining the wood
If bare wood is visible at the bottom of the scratch, you need to re-stain the wood. To remove damaged varnish, lightly roughen a small area around the scratch with sandpaper, steel wool or synthetic steel wool.

Find an oil-based stain that is a shade lighter than the wood finish. Stain the bare wood with a very small amount of stain on a rag, brush or cotton swab. If the color is too light, apply several coats. Rub away excess stain with a dry rag. If the wood becomes too dark, use a rag moistened in mineral sprits to lighten the wood. Then select a lighter color stain and continue.

WOOD FINISHING AND REPAIR

Several companies have simplified this repair process by putting oil-based wood stain into marker-like containers. You just rub the stain marker on the scratch. I suggest you start with a stain color that is lighter than the original finish, because torn and scratched wood fibers will absorb stain quickly and darken quickly. You can always apply a second coat if the color of the first coat is too light. Once the color is blended, patch the clear finish as described above and apply a wipe-on oil finish.

An oil finish is generally a good choice in refinishing, except over several coats of hard finish (see below), where it will just lie on the surface without hiding the scratches. Oil finish may work as a top coat over old varnish that has been cleaned or partially removed with refinisher chemicals.

Hard finishes
If the original finish was coated with polyurethane or urethane (hard, durable finishes typically used on tabletops, for example), scratches are difficult to repair. Recoating the whole surface won't work. The new coat may not adhere and might even magnify the scratches.

For small surface scratches that have not penetrated the stain or changed the color of the wood, carefully sand out the imperfection with 600 grit wet/dry sandpaper. Wet the sandpaper with water or lemon oil, and gently sand the damaged area. When you've removed the scratch, buff with 0000 steel wool and paste wax to bring back the shine.

You could also try oil finish to touch up a small scratch in polyurethane, but there are no guarantees of how the oil will stick or blend into the surface. However, you have little to lose by trying this method. Use an artist's brush to carefully fill the scratch, one thin coat at a time.

When a scratch has penetrated so deeply that a color difference is visible, you must fill the scratch and color the wood with one of many available products: oil stains, stain pens, or touch-up sticks. Use an artist's brush or toothpick to fill in tiny areas. After the material has dried, buff back the sheen with 0000 steel wool and paste wax.

If the piece is an antique, you may have to live with the scratch, or you might consult a furniture finish repair company.

Refinishing wood furniture

When refinishing furniture, once you've stripped off the old paint and sanded the wood, you have many, many options for finishing the surface. My preference is an oil-based stain and an oil rub-on finish. Visit a local paint store to review your options. Read the literature offered there.

I like oil-based stains because they penetrate the wood and are easy to control. I usually select several colors and test them before I do the whole project. After you test a small area, also test the clear finish over the dry stain. The finish will darken the stain color. Minwax, Zar and Sherwin Williams are brands I have used with success.

For a clear finish, try wipe-on or rub-on oil finishes like General Finishes, Zar or Minwax brands. These finishes are applied with a rag and have low odor. You can create any type of sheen or depth of finish. Applying more coats produces a deeper, glossier finish.

With wipe-on finishes, I like to apply several coats and allow the finish to dry fully. Then buff the finish with 0000 steel wool or a synthetic pad to remove all surface imperfections. Apply a final thin coat for a perfect finish.

WOOD FINISHING AND REPAIR

Use stripper pads, not steel wool

For aggressive removal of tough paints or buffing between coat of a clear finish, throw out your steel wool and use synthetic pads instead. I recommend a stripping pad made by 3M. This pad, about 4" x 11" and made of woven synthetic material, is designed to be used with chemical strippers. It doesn't fall apart like steel wool and will not poke through your gloves or stick in the wood grain. You can find this pad at most hardware and paint stores. It looks very much like the Scotch-Brite scouring pads used to clean your pots and pans.

3M also makes a synthetic steel wool in grades to match regular steel wool. You can remove rust, buff between coats, strip paint, or buff a final coat effectively with a synthetic pad.

Stripping paint from wood pores

Oak, walnut, ash and other woods have wide pores. It is difficult to remove old paint from the pores. Try these methods.

The first method is to spread a coat of chemical stripper, allow it to work the surface for several minutes, then scrub with a fingernail brush, a brass wire brush, or a 3M stripper pad.

The second method involves coating the area with a 50-50 mixture of shellac and alcohol. Let this dry on the finish. When you strip it off (it's easily removed), small particles of paint that have bonded to the shellac will lift out of the pores.

Finally, if you plan to stain the oak, remember that staining may cover some of these small paint particles. You'll need to experiment to see how well the stain covers. I have use darker stain to cover paint I could not remove.

Refinishing a damaged front door

Many homes feature a beautiful wood front door that is stained and varnished. In time, though, the varnish begins flaking and peeling, especially with no storm door.

Sunlight is the culprit. Ultraviolet (UV) rays attack the cellular structure of the wood under the varnish, giving it a "sunburn." Varnish can't stick to damaged wood. UV rays also damage the clear finish.

The best solution is to paint the door. Paint has coloring pigment that blocks UV rays and protects the wood. But if you really like that stained and varnished look, it requires a little work.

First you must sand, scrape or strip the damaged finish. Where the finish is in good condition, you must sand and roughen the surface.

How far you go with the refinishing depends on the condition of the door. If more than 25% of the finish is damaged, your best bet is to chemically strip the door and start with bare wood.

For a final clear finish, look for a UV-resistant varnish (often called spar varnish or marine finish). The finish is expensive and may only be available in a gloss formula. Follow the specific instructions for your varnish, and don't forget to finish all six areas of the door (front, back, top, bottom and sides).

A final option would be to install a storm door to protect the wood door. There are attractive storm doors available that are mostly glass so your wood door can still show through.

Removing stains from an oak floor

Refinishing oak floors is just like refinishing oak furniture. You can repair any type of imperfection without complete sanding (or stripping) and refinishing. However, often floors *are*

WOOD FINISHING AND REPAIR

sanded and refinished because this is the easiest route to a perfect new finish or because the homeowners want to lighten the whole surface. You need to decide whether repair or complete refinishing is in order for your floor.

If there is a light or faded area, try rubbing the spot with furniture refinisher on a steel wool pad. The strong solvent that will soften the existing clear finish and spread around a mixture of softened varnish and stain. This may even out the color variances. It might also lighten the whole surface as the old, darkened varnish is removed.

For dark stains, clean with a 50-50 solution of laundry bleach and water. Stains that disappear quickly were just surface mildew. Any remaining dark spots are water stains that have penetrated the wood. To remove these, sand the area or bleach it with wood bleach. Wood bleach is available at paint and hardware stores. It lightens the oak, turning it almost white.

After bleaching, the grain of the wood will be raised and rough. Smooth with sandpaper and then stain the area with an oil-based stain to match the original color. Finally, seal with the finish of your choice. I think wipe-on oil finishes are a good option for repairs.

You will need to be a bit of an artist with the stain color and final finish to blend in the color and gloss. Always start with a stain lighter than the final color you want to achieve. You can always add more stain or a darker color stain, but it is difficult to remove a dark stain color once it's in the wood grain. Also remember that the clear finish will make the stain color appear darker and richer.

You can see why floors are often re-sanded to remove imperfections. All stains, scratches, and damaged finish are removed with sanding, leaving the surface flat, smooth and ready for a new stain and clear finish. Sanding is the only way to ensure a like-new finish.

Safe finishes for children's wooden toys

The Toymakers line of finishes and dyes is made specifically for wood toys and is non-toxic once cured. The dyes are tinted with food coloring additives. The manufacturer claims that the finish is convenient to use and has a professional appearance. The clear finish is applied like an oil-based finish and has the look of high-quality varnish. The dyes come in four bright colors.

You can order the Toymakers finish by calling 1-(800)-279-4441. It's also available at some woodworkers' stores.

Several other manufacturers sell finishes that are safe when cured or dry. General Finishes is one such brand. You can also buy a special finish made for salad bowls and wood kitchen utensils. These clear finishes don't build up on the surface.

Lead is not used in paint anymore, but you should carefully read the safety precautions of any finish you select.

No need to oil or "feed" wood finishes

Despite what the advertisements say, lemon oil and similar products do not "feed" a wood finish. Lemon oil, a solvent-based cleaner, merely cleans the surface. The finish looks shinier because it's cleaner. Some products identified as lemon oil also contain furniture polish, which may further improve the appearance of the finish.

Check the label of the lemon oil container and you will find that it contains petroleum distillates. These oil-based cleaners can effectively remove built-up oil, dirt, and wax, but they

WOOD FINISHING AND REPAIR

don't oil the wood. It's a fallacy that lemon oil or other polishes feed the wood by returning oil to it. Most wood does not contain oil and never needs to be fed. Save the oil for the bearings on your furnace.

Chapter 4

CLEANING AND STAIN REMOVAL

My secret weapon for stain removal
I generally refer to Lift Off from Mostenbockers as my secret weapon for stain removal. The company provides specific stain removers for specific stain problems, stain removal kits, a travel kit, and larger spray containers.

The travel kit contains three chemicals designed for stains on virtually any surface, including auto interiors, fabric, dry marker boards, leather, nylon, plastic and more. Number 1 is intended for food, beverage and protein stains. Number 2 is used for adhesives, grease and oily stains, and tape. Number 3 is used for stains created by ink, markers and graffiti.

Also available are a Number 4 for spray paint and a Number 5 for latex-based stains.

All of these chemicals are packaged with a stain removal guide that helps you decide which chemical to use and how to remove stains from all types of fabric and hard surfaces. The guide also describes the best type of follow-up cleaning to eliminate any trace of the stain.

The kit is great, and the guide is a fantastic. Every household should have a stain removal kit on hand, because we never know when that emergency can happen.

The secret Mr. Fix-It window washing formula
To make a great formula for washing windows, combine the following:

> ½ cup sudsy ammonia
> 1 pint 70% isopropyl alcohol
> 1 teaspoon dishwashing detergent

- Add water to make one gallon.
- Tint the solution with food dye and pour it into a spray bottle. Label the container DANGEROUS CHEMICAL.
- Use this spray to dampen the windows. Then wipe them with a lint-free cloth.
- I use old dishcloths or paper towels.

Cleaning glass doors on a fireplace
Have you ever tried to clean the soot from glass fireplace doors? Tough, isn't it? Try using a cleaner specifically designed for removing soot and stains from fireplace glass, oven doors, and glass on wood-burning stoves.

Apply the product to the glass, allow it to work for a few minutes, and then wipe with a clean paper towel. To clean really messy glass, you may need to do two applications. Find this cleaner at fireplace stores.

Keeping a shower clean
Most people don't exactly relish scrubbing the tub or the shower walls. Here's my suggestion for doing the job once, then establishing a routine so heavy-duty cleanup won't be necessary so often.

Meticulously clean the shower and tub with a commercial

CLEANING AND STAIN REMOVAL

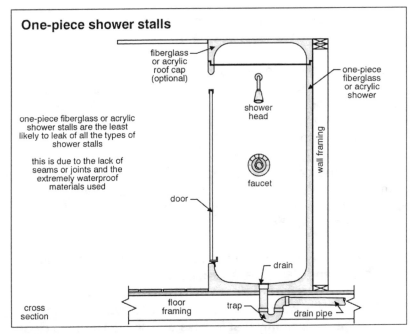

One-piece shower stalls

fiberglass or acrylic roof cap (optional)

one-piece fiberglass or acrylic shower

shower head

one-piece fiberglass or acrylic shower stalls are the least likely to leak of all the types of shower stalls

this is due to the lack of seams or joints and the extremely waterproof materials used

wall framing

faucet

door

drain

cross section

floor framing

trap

drain pipe

cleaner. Some of the better cleaners are Tilex and Comet Non-Abrasive Cleaner. Once the area shower is clean, all you need to do is wipe down the wet surfaces after a shower. Use a squeegee on flat surfaces and a towel on the rest. If water is wiped from the surface, there will be no water stains and no dirt buildup.

For vinyl or acrylic showers and tubs, you also can polish and finish with Gel-Gloss. This is a white, milky cleaner/polish much like automotive wax. With a little rubbing, it will remove most stains and discoloration. After it dries to a light powdery residue, buff with a clean cloth. This leaves a nice glossy protective finish that tends to mask scratches so the surface looks refinished.

Gel-Gloss also leaves a smooth, sealed surface that resists water spotting and stains by causing water to bead up and run off. If hard water stains are not present, dirt and mildew will not build up, and the tub stays clean.

You can also try a product called Clean Shower, which you lightly mist on the shower walls, glass door, curtain and fixtures after a shower. It makes water run off quickly so the shower stays clean. Clean Shower is inexpensive and is available in many stores.

Cleaning the bathtub and shower
I know there is always a better way to clean a bathtub. So I asked my radio listeners about their favorite products for this job. Here are their best ideas.

- Mrs. H --- I use rubbing alcohol (cheapest will do the job). This cleans glass, tile, and cupboard tops, too.

- Mary -- Why would anyone let an expensive plumbing fixture get so scummy that it takes drastic measures to clean it? Don't use soap to clean people. Use detergent bars— Olay, Zest, and Dove. They don't form scum, and drains don't require cleaning as often as with soap. There's still toothpaste to clean the tub.

- Arlene -- After trying every product on the grocery store shelves to clean my glass shower doors and ceramic tile shower, I followed the suggestion of the original installer and tried Bruce's Glass Stain Remover (Racy Enterprises, Fair Oaks, CA.). It is a slightly abrasive paste that removes water stains and lime buildup. They recommend using a scrubbing sponge with a slightly abrasive surface. It worked like a charm to remove buildup. When there is no lime buildup, I use X-14 Soap Scum Remover (Block Drug Co., Inc., Jersey City, NJ) in a spray form. Finding the right product is touchy because many shower doors, mine included, have a polished aluminum frame and track.

CLEANING AND STAIN REMOVAL

The wrong product can ruin the finish of the metal.

- Virginia --- I use fabric softener to keep my bathtub and tub doors clean. It seems to keep scum from forming.

- Frank --- Every time we use the shower and tub, we wipe it down with a towel. After 30 years, the tub and tile still look like new and never require drastic cleaning with chemicals.

And finally: for rust stains, try Zud. You'll find it in most grocery stores. It is an abrasive cleaner with oxalic acid, a strong oxidizer that removes rust. Dampen the rust stain and make a paste of Zud and water. Allow it to sit on the stain for several hours. If it dries out, add more water and cover it with plastic to stop evaporation. Zud should remove the rust with little scrubbing.

Whink is also an excellent rust stain remover. You can find Whink in grocery stores.

Removing hard water stains from a glass shower door
The most common type of stain on glass shower doors results when hard water scale dries on the surface. The scale attracts dirt, soap scum, and mildew.

To remove this buildup, try cleaners made for hard water scale or lime removal. Such cleaners list in their ingredients an acid such as sulfamic, hydroxyacetic, citrus or maleic. Comet, Whink and Zud all have lime and scale removers.

Follow the direction for the cleaner you select, and allow time for the cleaner to work. The acid will react with the hard water deposits to remove them. If these cleaners fail, you could try an acid-based toilet bowl cleaner. Remember to follow all safety precautions. These strong cleaners will not harm the glass but may dull or harm the metal trim and gaskets around the shower door and frame.

It's best to maintain a clean shower stall and glass by wiping down the surfaces after the last shower of the day. If water dries on the surface, hard water scale will form.

Grout - keeping it clean
It can be quite a challenge to keep the grout clean on bathroom walls and floors or kitchen counters. Since grout is porous, stains easily penetrate and can become difficult or even impossible to remove.

For existing grout, apply a sealer. Sealer helps make the grout resistant to stains and will also aid in cleaning. Most sealers are applied to the grout lines and allowed to dry for several days before use.

When installing new tile, help hide future stains by using grout that's off-white or cement gray—a very forgiving color. Pure white or black grout can create big problems.

Removing hair spray buildup from bathroom surfaces
Hair spray can leave white spots on bathroom surfaces. To remove them, wet a rough rag with rubbing alcohol or denatured alcohol. You may need to soak the areas and rub more than once over several minutes to remove the deposits.

An ammonia-based cleaner will often work, too. Use sudsy ammonia or a similar cleaner.

If alcohol or ammonia cleaners do not do the trick, try Goof-Off, Goo-Gone, or Oops. These are stronger solvent cleaners. They are flammable, so use them only in a well ventilated area away from any source of combustion. Normally, these solvent cleaners will not harm stained and varnished wood-work unless the varnish is soft. Test in an inconspicuous area first. These solvents will not harm hardware.

To remove the deposits from smooth hardware, try simply scraping the deposits with a vinyl scraper or even a fingernail.

Cleaning old porcelain bathroom fixtures

If your home has old porcelain sinks, toilets and/or bathtubs, ordinary bathroom cleaners may not remove stains from them. You need powerful chemical cleaners to cut dirt, stains and deposits.

Visit a commercial cleaning supply company. Explain your problem, and they can provide strong chemicals. You MUST follow label directions and safety precautions.

For a porcelain toilet and tub, you can use a cleaner with acid content. The acid will cut through the hard water stains that instigate all bathroom cleaning problems. The cleaner will re-move dirt and stains along with the hard water deposits.

Strong chemicals available at most grocery stores include Tilex, Scum Cutter, The Works, and Sno Bol.

If abrasive cleansers have roughened the stained areas, they will be almost impossible to keep clean. Once the smooth porcelain surface is roughened, it continues to attract dirt.

Cleaning white film from coffeemaker

Over time, a white film can build up in a coffeemaker from hard water deposits (even if you have a water softener). I have found that the coffeemaker cleaners work well. I use a cleaner from Whink that you can find in most grocery stores. Mix the cleaner with water and fill the reservoir.

Brew the solution through the coffeemaker into the decanter.
Rinse the coffeemaker twice by cycling clear water through
the brew cycle before you use it for coffee. I also use the
chemical brew to clean decanters and worn coffee mugs.

The product uses acids to dissolve hard water deposits, so
follow label instructions carefully and avoid skin or eye contact.

Banish stains around cabinet door handles
If your cabinets are varnished wood, the stains around the
door handles are a combination of softened varnish, oil from
the skin, and dirt. Tackle them with a product like Goo-Gone
or Oops. These strong solvents dissolve the stains and the
softened varnish. Mineral spirits may also work.

Use a small amount on a coarse cloth, and apply it to the
stain. Test the cleaner on an inconspicuous area first, because it may affect the color of the wood under the clear finish. As the stain is softened, scrub to wipe it away. Go at the
marks slowly, since you are removing a thin layer of softened
varnish. Remove as little as possible.

After removing stains, revarnish if needed. Or use an oil finish
like Minwax Antique Oil or General Finishes Wipe-On Oil.
Both of these work over any finish. They are applied with a
rag, are easy to control, and have little odor.

Restoring Formica countertops
It is impossible to restore the color and eliminate scratches
from plastic laminate (brand name: Formica). The same properties that make plastic laminate durable also make it impossible to patch or repair.

However, you can clean and polish laminate with a product
like Gel-Gloss. This is a white, milky cleaner/polish much like

automotive wax. With a little rubbing, Gel-Gloss will remove most stains and discoloration. After it dries to a light powdery residue, buff with a clean cloth.

This leaves a nice glossy protective finish that tends to mask scratches so that the plastic laminate looks refinished. It also leaves a smooth, sealed surface that resists water spotting and stains. In the future, if the counter gets dull, apply more.

Never use bleach or abrasive cleaners on plastic laminates. They can damage the surface.

Removing Super Glue from a countertop
If Super Glue or a similar product is spilled on a countertop, the solution is simple. Super Glue remover is available at larger hardware stores.

Removing marker stains from paint and woodwork
If a youngster armed with an indelible marker has created "artwork" on surfaces in your home, the way to remove the marks depends on the surface.

For a painted surface, any cleaner strong enough to remove the marker stain will also remove the paint. I suggest you prime the area with BIN until the stain is gone or is just a ghost. Then paint with normal latex wall paint. The primer is the key to covering the stain.

For stained and varnished wood, try Oops, Goof-Off or Lift Off. These strong solvent cleaners can remove the marker without damaging sturdy varnish. Dampen the stain and gently rub with a rag dampened with the cleaner. Treat until the stain is gone. Follow the safety precautions for these cleaners, provide plenty of ventilation, and do not use them near open flame.

If the cleaner dulls the varnish, renew it with wipe-on oil finish like tung oil or any other type. These will stick to the existing finish, and you can control the application with a rag. Most finishes are gloss or satin; pick the shine to match your existing finish. You can also add extra coats for more depth and gloss.

If the marker stain has penetrated into the wood, you will need to refinish or replace the wood.

Removing a white ring from a wooden coffee table

A white ring on a wooden coffee table is caused by moisture absorbed into the table's clear finish. Professional refinishers call this effect "blooming." Most blooming can be removed by rubbing with mild abrasive to remove a thin coat of finish in the white area. Use automobile polishing compound, rotten-stone and mineral spirits, 0000 steel wool, or even cigar ashes and mineral spirits.

Carefully rub the area with the abrasive until the white bloom disappears. Be careful, and go slowly. It may take quite a bit of rubbing. Since this removes a fraction of the surface finish, you must re-wax the surface to touch up the gloss. You may even need to touch up the finish if the bloom was deep. Consider using oil finish for a touch-up.

The good news is that a white bloom is usually only in the clear surface finish. A darker stain indicates wood damage below the surface and could require complete refinishing.

Removing stains from marble

Marble looks tough, but unfortunately it is fairly porous and tends to stain easily. Stain removal may require professional help. Strong cleaners can damage marble.

Stain removal will probably involve using a poultice that combines a cleaning chemical with whiting or talc, forming a thick,

CLEANING AND STAIN REMOVAL

plaster-like paste. The stain is drawn into the paste. Different types of stains require different types of chemicals.

After stains are removed, marble can be polished with a marble-polishing powder and buffing pad. This usually requires power equipment.

Sound complicated? It is. Information on marble cleaning, stain removal, polishing and related maintenance products is available from Gawet Marble and Granite or from Renaissance Products.

Removing masking tape
Have you ever left cheap masking tape on too long until it becomes welded to the surface? When you peel it off, residue remains. On glass, a razor blade can remove this residue, but what can you use on other surfaces?

Try removing "welded" masking tape by heating it with a hair dryer. Warm the tape for a few minutes and use a sharp scraper or razor blade to lift a corner. Continue to heat the tape as you pull it from the surface. Draw the tape back against itself to aid in removal.

You can remove residual adhesive with mineral spirits or waterless hand cleaner (the type auto mechanics use). Spread cleaner on the surface and let it work for a while. Then scrape off the residue.

Removing old shelf paper
Shelf paper should have never been invented - well, OK, it should never be used. But if it's on your shelves, how do you get rid of it?

Heat the shelf paper with a hair dryer. Slowly warm the surface and pull up a corner as the adhesive is softened. As you lift, you can also apply warm water and detergent to soften the material.

To remove the adhesive residue, try a solution of Mex cleaner and water, waterless hand cleaner, WD40, or even dry cleaning fluid. If you use a flammable cleaner, follow label directions, use plenty of ventilation, and keep it away from any source of combustion.

Cleaning and polishing brass-colored metal

Brass can have a beautiful finish, but over time it acquires black stains. Some brass finishes are just a coating and not really brass. If you'd like to restore such a surface, first you have to determine whether the metal is ferrous (iron or steel) or brass.

Test it with a magnet. A magnet will stick to iron or steel but not to copper or brass. If it looks like brass but the magnet sticks, it might have been coated, plated or painted.

Assuming you have brass parts, clean the brass with a commercial cleaner. This requires a trip to a good hardware store or to a commercial cleaning supplier.

Gillespie, Brasso, Flitz and others make brass cleaners. Most require coating the brass with a strong cleanser, then polishing and rubbing.

After the brass is clean and polished, some cleaning products require a neutralizer. Once the brass is clean, you can also coat it with clear lacquer or acrylic to prevent future tarnishing.

Cleaning a stone fireplace

Lannon stone or any light colored stone or brick fireplaces can get dirty from smoke residue over the years. I recom-

CLEANING AND STAIN REMOVAL

mend having the fireplace cleaned by a chimney sweep. These professionals use special chemicals to remove soot from brick and stone.

You can also consult contractors that clean acoustical tile. Find them in the Yellow Pages under Acoustical Tile Cleaning. They have special cleaning chemicals that can remove and lighten soot stains.

If you want to try cleaning the stone yourself, use a heavy duty detergent like Mex or TSP substitute and a few ounces of bleach per gallon of warm water. Soak the area with the solution and scrub with a brush. Rinse well.

You must use lots of water to raise the dirt to the surface of the porous stone or brick. Have plenty of dropcloths and towels on hand to catch the dirty water. Wear skin and eye protection. You may have to clean the surface several times.

If stains remain, you can remove them with a poultice of dry laundry detergent and water or heavy duty cleaner, bleach and diatomaceous earth. A poultice is a paste that you apply to a stain and leave in place as the stain is slowly dissolved and absorbed. Bleach may whiten the surface, so use it sparingly.

Finally, you can try using a "dry sponge" to clean the stone. Dry sponges are sold at commercial cleaning-supply stores, lighting stores that sell lampshades, and some wallpaper stores. A dry sponge is essentially a soft spongy eraser. As you rub it on, it absorbs the stain. Dry sponges are often used to remove soot in fire restoration projects. They also clean lampshades and wallpaper. Dry Magic is one brand of dry sponge.

Just Fix It

Chapter 5

HEATING AND AIR CONDITIONING

Understanding your forced-air furnace

During normal operation, the burner on the furnace starts up, warming the heat exchanger and the air in and around the heat exchanger. When the air is warm, a fan control starts the fan to distribute the warm air into your home. This delay is built in so the fan does not start immediately and blow cold air on your feet.

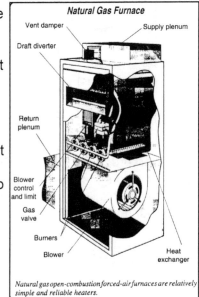

Natural Gas Furnace

Vent damper
Supply plenum
Draft diverter
Return plenum
Blower control and limit
Gas valve
Burners
Blower
Heat exchanger

When the room air near the thermostat is warmed to the set point, the thermostat turns the burner off. The fan continues to run until it has removed the heat from the heat exchanger. When the heat exchanger is cool, the fan limit control turns the fan off.

Natural gas open-combustion forced-air furnaces are relatively simple and reliable heaters.

Occasionally, the fan may start up again within a few minutes and cycle for another 40 seconds or so. If this is the case, your fan control limit switch is set to such a low temperature that it senses residual heat in the metal of the heat exchanger, so it re-starts the fan.

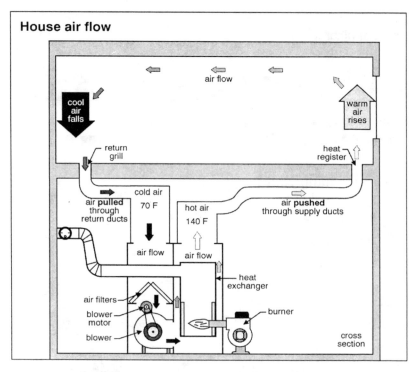

House air flow

This low setting helps utilize all the heat in the heat exchanger. It does cause some extra wear and tear on the fan, but that should not be a major concern. A heating contractor can adjust this control so the fan does not start a second time, but then you will lose some heat.

High-efficiency gas furnaces feel cooler
High-efficiency gas furnaces discharge cooler air into living spaces compared to older furnaces. You'll get used to the cooler temperature, and the energy savings of up to 40 percent should help "temper" your feelings toward the new furnace. Because your new furnace is more efficient, you may wish to raise the temperature setting a few degrees, allowing more comfort at little additional cost.

HEATING AND AIR CONDITIONING

The discharge temperature is lower because the furnace uses almost all of the available energy in the gas it burns. This lowers the temperature that's required to transfer heat from the products of combustion into the air circulated in your home.

You may feel a draft as this cooler air discharges at a greater speed from the supply duct grills. If this draft is a major problem, consider installing a plastic air deflector to redirect the air discharge. If air is not directed toward your skin, you will not feel a draft.

Another possibility: ask your heating contractor to check that the furnace and the fan speed were set up properly. If you notice a draft at one particular register, the contractor can lower the flow to that register.

Some top-of-the-line furnaces also have variable-speed fans and variable heating rates to adjust for this "draft" problem. Have the contractor make sure that all the settings are correct.

When a high-efficiency furnace stops producing heat
Furnaces vented with plastic pipes can have simple but serious "no heat" problems in the winter. If snow or ice blocks the pipes, the furnace will not run. Keep the vent pipes clear, and check them if your furnace will not run. If pipes are packed with snow or frost, use a hair dryer to thaw out the buildup.

Heating and cooling adjustments—forced air furnace
Warm air rises; cooler air sinks. Keep this principle in mind, and you'll realize why opening the correct air returns in winter and summer will provide better air distribution—which, in turn, allows more even temperatures in your home.

When you use a forced air furnace for summer cooling, you should open the *high* returns. This allows the furnace to take

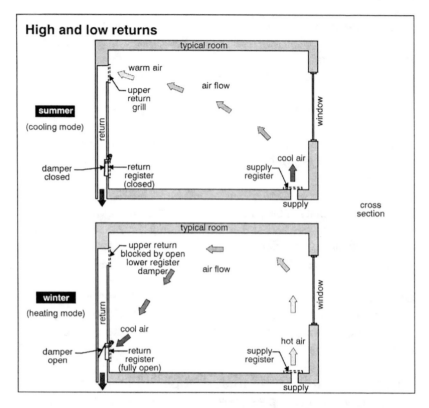

High and low returns

typical room

warm air

upper return grill

air flow

summer

(cooling mode)

cool air

damper closed

return register (closed)

supply register

supply

cross section

window

return

typical room

upper return blocked by open lower register damper

air flow

winter

(heating mode)

cool air

hot air

damper open

return register (fully open)

supply register

supply

window

return

warmer air from the top of the room back to the air condition-ing cooling coil in the furnace. In the winter, open the *low* re-turns to collect cold air at the floor.

For a two-story home, you may also need to adjust the *supply* air for winter and summer. In the winter, warm air rises to the second floor, so less heating is required there.

In the summer, warm air still rises, and a hot attic adds even more heat, so you need greater cooling (air flow) to the sec-ond floor than to the first floor.

The best way to control air flow is to adjust the small dampers

HEATING AND AIR CONDITIONING

in the heating/cooling duct system in the basement. Often, these dampers are found where round supply duct runs connect to the main (rectangular) ducts.

Look for small (¼-inch) threaded rods and wing nuts. You can adjust the damper by turning the screwdriver slot on the small rod. When the slot is parallel to the duct, the damper is fully open. You don't need to adjust the wing nut, which simply locks the rod into place.

Heating ducts vary. Some systems have levers indicating the direction of the damper. Some rectangular ducts have dampers and levers.

To adjust air flow for summer cooling, start by fully opening all second floor dampers. Next, partially close dampers to first floor rooms that are getting lots of cold air. You will find that closing the damper to 50% or turning the shaft to 45 degrees will only partially slow the air flow. Often, even if you fully close the damper, there will still be air flow because the dampers fit very loosely in the ducts.

Closing first floor dampers will direct air to the second floor. Mark your damper settings for summer and winter once you have found the correct balance. Remember to clean the furnace filter, too. A plugged filter can also restrict air flow.

Older homes were not built for cooling—the supply and return ducts to the second floor may not be adequate—so adjustments may not solve the problem. A quick fix may be to run the furnace fan continuously.

Furnace air filters and maintenance
How often should you change the filter on the furnace? Whenever it's dirty. And although it sounds silly, better filters get dirty more quickly and need to be changed more often.

Just Fix It **Tom Feiza - Mr. Fix-It**

A standard cheap (about $1) fiberglass air filter should be checked once a month and changed when it shows visible dirt. You also need to check the filter when running the central air conditioner, because air circulates through the furnace and the filter.

I suggest you replace the cheap fiberglass filter with a pleated paper filter. You will find them in any hardware or building supply store next to the standard filters. Read the label - some are more efficient than others. Price will vary from about $3 to $15. These filters will trap much more dirt and smaller particles of dirt. They need to be changed more often because they do a better job of trapping dirt.

The next level up from standard throw-away filters are washable filters and electrostatic washable filters. Washable foam filters work quite well if coated with a special sticky spray

Replacing and Cleaning Filters

Filter

Some furnace filters, held in place by a wire rack, wrap around the inside of the fan blower compartment.

Some filters insert into a slot in the return air duct. The slot should be sealed with duct tape between filter changes.

Some filters are located in filter grills in return air registers

HEATING AND AIR CONDITIONING

like Filter Coat. Electrostatic filters are relatively expensive (about $100), but they do trap dirt well.

A better filter is the 6-inch-thick pleated paper filter. Air is forced through a long accordion of filter paper. Fine holes in the paper trap small particles of dirt. The large surface area limits pressure loss in the heating system. A special frame needs to be installed in the duct work, and the filter costs about $25, but it will last one or two years.

The top of the line is an electronic filter that charges metal plates in the air stream and attracts dust. This is the only type of filter that removes smoke particles from the air. This filter costs about $700 installed. Filter plates must be washed monthly in the dishwasher or by hand with soapy water.

I consider the pleated paper filters a good investment. The more expensive electronic filters are great for people with allergies or sensitivity to dust.

Service requirements for older furnaces

If your warm air furnace is old (say, 20 years or older), I suggest you have a professional heating contractor service it every year. This is your best protection against carbon monoxide dangers and heating problems. Routine service will also ensure peak efficiency to save you operating costs.

A good service and inspection costs about $80 and should include a complete cleaning, safety check, and tuning. The service contractor should:

- clean the burner and heat exchanger, and inspect for cracks.
- remove the burners, clean them, and tune for proper combustion.
- perform a carbon monoxide test in the heat exchanger.

- check the vent pipe and draft diverter.
- inspect the chimney for obstructions and draft.
- check vent pipes for proper clearance and materials.
- test fan controls and safety controls.
- check the thermostat.
- run the furnace through a complete cycle.
- check flame roll-out.
- check gas pressure (if appropriate for your furnace).
- clean and adjust the pilot light assembly.
- inspect gas fittings and repair any leaks.
- lubricate the fan and motor.
- check belt condition and tension.
- service the filter.
- clean the fan and housing if excessive dirt has accumu-lated.

Replacing parts or cleaning extensively will cost extra.

You should have a basic understanding of how the system works, so ask the service contractor to explain the basics. You should routinely service the filter and lubricate the fan and motor a second time during the heating season. You should also inspect the flue connection to the chimney.

Noises from the heating/cooling system
You may have noticed unexplained noises from your central heating/cooling system. What causes them, and what can you do about them?

A typical problem: when the air conditioning starts, there is often a loud "pop" from the ductwork. This may not occur when the furnace switches on.

When the central air conditioning runs, the furnace fan must move more air through the system than when the unit is used for heating. Often the fan will automatically run at a higher

HEATING AND AIR CONDITIONING

speed for greater volume and pressure.

Because of this increased pressure, the duct work is more likely to pop outward slightly. You can locate the problem area by listening for the sound and watching the ductwork when the air conditioner starts up. You'll probably notice movement and sound in the large, flat pieces of sheet metal near the furnace.

When you find the duct that is moving or popping, reinforce it with a small brace—screw a lightweight angle iron into the sheet metal over the part that is moving.

Now, how about noises you hear from your forced-air furnace? When the heating system starts and runs for a few minutes, there is often clicking and slight pounding of the ductwork in the basement.

This problem occurs as the metal ductwork heats up. The expanding metal needs room to move. The ductwork is trapped between the framing members of the house. Watch and listen for the problem area(s) as the furnace runs. You may need to loosen mounting brackets or adjust ductwork that is forced against wood framing.

Use your windows to help your air conditioner

Storm windows work as well in the summer as they do in the winter. Closing your storms will reduce the gain of heat through the windows and will also help stop infiltration of hot air. If possible, close shades and blinds to block direct sun.

Central air conditioner, part 1: to cover or not to cover?

Your central air conditioning unit consists of a compressor and condensing unit placed outdoors in a metal housing. These units, built to resist the weather, generally do not need a cover. In fact, covers can cause problems because they trap moisture and create an inviting winter home for small animals.

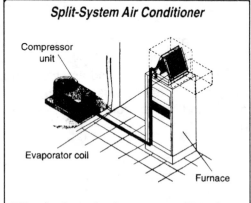

Split-System Air Conditioner

Compressor unit

Evaporator coil

Furnace

This upflow furnace has the evaporator coil in its plenum. The condenser and compressor are outdoors in their own cabinet. Split system air conditioners can be a part of combustion furnaces, electric furnaces, or heat pumps.

Professionals who service the units tell me that most of the damage they see in spring was caused by rodents living in the units and chewing on wiring.

If your air conditioner is subject to falling ice or other debris, you could cover its top with a piece of plywood, plastic or metal held in place by a weight.

Central air conditioner, part 2: seasonal shutdown and re-starting
Central air conditioning systems are relatively maintenance free, but you do need to take several precautions to prevent problems.

Autumn
In autumn, when the cooling season ends, turn off the power to your air conditioning unit either at the circuit breaker or at the electrical disconnect near the unit. This saves energy by turning off a small crankcase heater inside the unit. Thus, your air conditioner will be less likely to attract small animals during cold weather.

Turning off the power also prevents accidental starting during the winter, which could ruin the compressor.

HEATING AND AIR CONDITIONING

Spring
In the spring, follow these steps:

1. If you placed a plywood cover on the unit the previous autumn, remove it now.

2. Check that the coils and fan are clean. If necessary, clean them with a hose and a soft brush. Make sure that the main power to the unit is still turned off when you do this.

3. Inspect the unit. It should be level. Plants must not obstruct air flow; they should be 12 inches from the side of the unit and 36 inches from the air discharge.

4. The outdoor temperature should be 65 degrees or higher for 24 hours before you operate the unit.

5. Turn on the power to the unit at least 24 hours before operating the system. This gives the crankcase heater time to warm up the unit if needed. The heater warms the compressor crankcase, ensuring that oil is separated from refrigerant. When you turn the power on, make sure the thermostat control is set to keep the air conditioner off. Running the unit in cold weather can ruin the compressor.

Central air conditioning will drain water from a pan in ductwork above the furnace, so check that the hose is clear and directed to the floor drain.

The central air system is a big investment. If you have any doubts, have a professional service the unit and walk through the start-up with you.

What does a "ton" of air conditioning mean?
When dealers and contractors talk about "tons" of cooling in central air conditioning systems, what do they mean?

The term came into use when engineers developed standards for measuring mechanical cooling capacity. At that time, ice was commonly used for cooling. Engineer Joe Cool decided that cooling capacity measurements should relate to ice melting.

The standard was set equating one "ton" of cooling to the amount of energy needed to melt one ton (2000 lbs.) of ice over a 24-hour period.

For the technically competent, the exact figure for one ton of cooling is 12,000 Btu per hour. (Btu stands for British thermal unit, a measurement of heat or energy.) When ice changes from solid to liquid, the change of phase requires 144 Btu per pound or 288,000

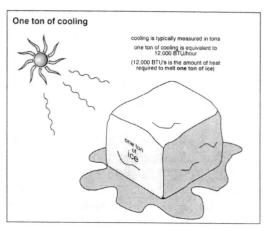

One ton of cooling

cooling is typically measured in tons
one ton of cooling is equivalent to 12,000 BTU/hour
(12,000 BTU's is the amount of heat required to melt one ton of ice)

one ton of ice

Btu per 2,000 lbs. When melted in 24 hours, the 288,000 is divided by 24 hours and equals 12,000 Btu per hour.

Rerouting a hose that drains your heating/cooling system
Let's say you have central air conditioning and a high-efficiency furnace. Both of these produce water that drains through a flexible tube extending way across the basement to a floor drain. You're worried that someone might trip on the hose. How can you fix this hazard?

You can't totally eliminate the hose, because the water must be drained. But you can re-route the hose overhead, then drop it down to a laundry tub or floor drain.

To do this, you'll need a small pump and container unit specifically designed for condensate. Its water tank - about the size of a large lunch bucket - is placed next to the furnace. As water collects, a 110-volt pump inside the tank automatically pumps the water out to any proper water receptacle.

You can purchase this equipment from a heating/air conditioning dealer. You will need to route the hose into the small tank, install the drain line, and provide a 110 volt (standard) outlet near the pump.

Reducing severe dampness throughout the house
During winter, some homes have problems with excessive moisture. It's most noticeable as condensation ("steam") on windows. If moisture is excessive and stays on your windows for several days...if water runs off windows and damages wood surfaces...if ice forms on windows and frames...or if storm windows remained fogged up and icy all winter, you need to reduce the humidity level inside your home.

Condensation requires a cool surface and moisture in the air. Inside your home, when the temperature of the glass drops below the dew point of the inside air, invisible water vapor in the air condenses on the cool glass. More condensation occurs when there is more water vapor in the air and/or when glass surfaces become colder.

Evaluate changes you have made to your home—any effort to tighten up a home and reduce air infiltration will increase humidity levels. A high-efficiency furnace vented with two plastic pipes draws combustion air from outside and reduces ventilation. Weatherstripping, better windows, caulking, and any other measures you have taken to reduce air leaks will increase the amount of moisture retained inside your home.

Try to increase ventilation by running kitchen and bath exhaust fans whenever steam is produced by cooking or bathing/showering. In the bathroom, keep the fan running until the bathroom is dry. Add timer switches to the fans if needed.

Limit the number of plants in your home. Look for plumbing leaks or damp areas in the basement. If basement crawl spaces have bare soil, cover the soil with a vapor barrier.

There are many other sources of moisture and ways to eliminate excess moisture. Often your local natural gas utility company can provide information on moisture problems. University extensions often have good booklets on solving moisture problems.

Reducing basement dampness in the summer
There are several ways of reducing dampness in your basement during the summer.

If you have central air conditioning and the supply/return ducts are connected to the basement, you can air condition the space. This will remove humidity and will mix basement air with overall home air. There will be a marginal cost for this, but the basement is cool already, and most of the energy will go toward removing the humidity.

If you don't have air conditioning but there is central hot air heat and ductwork connected to the basement, you can run the furnace fan to ventilate the basement. Mixing the upstairs air, which is drier, with the basement air will help dry out the basement. This is an inexpensive option.

If there is no ductwork in the basement, consider opening basement windows on dry days to ventilate the area. Open at least two windows and run a fan in one of them to speed up the process. When it is humid outside, close the windows. Your final option is to run a dehumidifier in the basement. In

HEATING AND AIR CONDITIONING

this case, do not ventilate the basement; allow the dehumidifier to remove the moisture. A dehumidifier works by moving
moist air across a coil (similar to an air conditioner) where the
moisture condenses into liquid.

Remember that mechanical refrigeration with a dehumidifier is
relatively expensive compared to natural ventilation. It takes
almost 1000 Btu to condense one pound of water from water
vapor. This can be more expensive than a refrigerator.

I prefer to open the windows and use natural ventilation. This
allows the basement to air out so that it smells like the great
outdoors.

Heating a basement recreation room

The best heating system for a basement recreation room is a
connection to the central forced-air heating system. This provides both heat and ventilation. However, a common problem
is that the basement remains about 10 degrees cooler than
the rest of the house. A little supplemental heat is in order.

During sunny, cool weather, as the first floor experiences heat
gain from windows, the furnace will not run. This makes the
basement area cooler because it needs a small amount of
heat but has no gain from windows. For a quick solution, try
running the fan on the central system. This will bring warmer
air to the basement.

The best solution is to add supplemental electric resistance
heat in the basement room. This could be a portable heater or
permanently mounted baseboards. Either will work.

The advantage of the electric heat is you can run it only when
you need it. You will also find that it takes little additional heat
to warm the room because the basement has little heat loss.
Once it is warm, it will stay warm.

Before you add electric heat, check any existing heating ducts (for instance, for a finished basement room, you may have added ducts that extend from the existing ducts). One duct should be a supply and one should be a return. Add a return if you don't have one—it is hard for your furnace to blow air into a sealed box. You could also adjust the dampers in the ducts to direct more air into the basement.

Excessive winter dryness indoors

Humidification of air inside the home has been the subject of many articles and investigations. Manufactures of humidifiers have claimed that humidified air would protect us from health hazards, but there are no firm facts that humidified air is better for us. In fact, humidifiers can cause problems with excessive moisture and even mold or bacteria.

To decide on the need for a humidifier, evaluate the comfort of your home during the dead of winter. Many of today's tighter, energy-efficient homes don't need additional moisture. Condensation on windows indicates excessive humidity; in that case, you don't need a humidifier. However, if your nose and skin are dry, and static electricity is a problem, you may need a humidifier.

The best type is a central humidifier that mounts on a forced-air furnace. Look for one that flushes water over a panel and drains away excess water as it operates. It should be mounted on the return duct to prevent water leaks into the furnace, and it should have a humidistat control that automatically turns on the unit as needed.

Aprilaire is a quality brand of furnace-mounted humidifier. Its newer models have a removable plastic cover that makes the unit easy to maintain. This type flushes water over a panel and doesn't require a water reservoir.

HEATING AND AIR CONDITIONING

Portable humidifiers can operate with a reservoir and evaporative panel. To create mist, some use ultrasound, others use a spinning wheel (for a cool mist), and others use heat (making steam). I consider all of these types hard to maintain and difficult to control. Any unit with a water reservoir is a potential source of mold or bacteria and must be meticulously cleaned and disinfected on a routine basis.

Chapter 6

APPLIANCES

Clean those refrigerator coils

It's important to clean the refrigerator coils once or twice per year. The refrigerator will run less, use less electricity, operate more efficiently, and last longer.

The refrigerator has a compressor that forces refrigerant through coils in the freezer and on the refrigerator's exterior. Evaporator coils in the freezer remove heat from inside. This heat is emitted into the room through the exterior condenser coils.

The coils look like thin tubes, sometimes with connecting fins like a radiator on your car. Some coils are mounted at the rear of the refrigerator. Other are located below the refrigerator, where a fan moves air across the coil. When you stand next to the refrigerator in the winter and feel a warm breeze at your feet, it means the condenser coil and fan are working.

If the exterior condenser coils become dirty, they are less efficient at transferring heat into the air around the refrigerator.

To clean the coils, carefully vacuum them. Remove stubborn dust with a soft brush. You can even buy a coil cleaning brush at a hardware store.

If your refrigerator has coils and a fan below the refrigerator, you will need to remove some access panels to reach the coils. I suggest you follow the specific instructions for your refrigerator and unplug the unit before you attempt to clean the coils.

Cleaning is simple. You will be amazed at how much lint and dust has collected on the coils. If you have pets, you need to clean the coil more often.

When moving a refrigerator, wait a while before restarting.

According to service information provided by Whirlpool, it makes a difference how a freezer, refrigerator or icemaker is transported. If the appliance is moved on its side or back, it must stand upright for 24 hours before being restarted. If the unit is transported upright, it may be restarted immediately.

Why? Lubricating oil for the refrigeration compressor can flow out of the crankcase if the unit is not upright. Running the unit without oil can ruin the compressor, which is a major problem.

Repairing balky gas stovetop burners

Over time, the burners of a gas stove may refuse to light automatically, even though the pilot light is on. This usually means that the burners and/or the small tubes that transfer gas to the burners are dirty or plugged.

Remove the burner covers. Clean the burners with detergent on a damp rag. For hardened deposits, you may need to scrub with an abrasive pad. If the holes are blocked, clear them with a toothpick or a wire brush.

If this does not solve the problem, check the tubes. Raise the metal cover of the stove. (The cover is usually hinged at the rear so you can lift the front.) You will see little tubes leading from the burners to one or two pilot lights. Often the tubes can be removed for cleaning.

APPLIANCES

Touch-ups make appliances look like new
You can touch up small nicks and scratches on appliances with special touch-up paint available in most hardware stores. It comes in a small container that looks like a bottle of finger-nail polish.

Before applying the paint, you may need to lightly sand the damaged area to roughen the surface and remove any rust. Don't sand the surrounding surface. Clean the area with a rough rag and some paint thinner, then allow it to dry.

The touch-ups will make your appliances look like new.

Painting metal finishes of interior furnishings
For metal cabinets, appliances or office furniture, you can obtain a factory-like finish with electrostatic painting. This method uses an electrostatic charge between the metal and the paint to achieve an excellent finish without overspray. Less masking is required, and there is little waste. Odor is also reduced because less paint is used.

Look under "Appliance Painting and Refinishing" in the Yellow Pages. Make sure that you get the electrostatic (magnetic) spray and that high quality paint is used. Some contractors use an epoxy spray that is very durable. A quality job involves careful surface cleaning and preparation.

It will cost about $250 to restore one item, or less per item if several are painted. The work is usually done in your home in one day and is worth the price to restore a quality piece in good condition.

Rust on dishwasher racks? Act now!
If you've noticed rusty spots on the racks inside your dish-washer, I suggest you touch these up before the problem grows into a bigger job.

A friend of mine found that Guardcote Touch Up Paint does the job quite well. This paint is designed to be safe in the dishwasher and to hold up under harsh dishwasher conditions.

The container has its own brush, and you apply paint to a clean surface. Allow it to dry for 24 hours. If additional coats are required, allow 30 minutes between coats. Various colors are available: blue, white, green, almond, or clear.

Chapter 7

LIGHTING

When a fluorescent light buzzes
Humming or buzzing in a fluorescent light fixture is usually caused by a ballast that's poorly built or improperly mounted. The hum occurs as electrical current moves through metal plates in the ballast.

With the power off, open the fixture. The ballast is a metal box about 2 by 3 by 10 inches with wires leading to it. Make sure that the mounting screws are tight. If there are vibration-isolation spacers, check them. Compare this bad fixture to any similar quiet fixtures you may have to identify the problem. It may be necessary to replace the ballast.

Also check to make sure that the framing of the fixture is not amplifying the sound. You may need to change the mounting.

Burning odor from light fixture or outlet
If a light fixture gives off a burning smell, disconnect the fixture until you have determined the source of the odor. Overheating electrical wires and devices often emit a burning smell. Don't use the fixture again until a professional has repaired it.

A fluorescent fixture may have a ballast that has failed and is spilling tar. For typical incandescent light fixtures, the burning smell may occur if you're using an oversized bulb. Check the rating of the fixture and the wattage of the bulb. The rating will be inside the fixture, near the bulb. Never exceed the wattage recommended.

You might also have a loose electrical connection at the splice or in the outlet box, or a loose screw or lamp base. A loose connection can create excessive resistance to electrical flow, and the resistance causes heat.

Excessive heat makes metal connections expand and con-tract, loosening them further. This heat can damage insulation and even start a fire. Sometimes, when such excessive heat melts plastic, the problem area emits a misleading "dead ani-mal" smell.

If you notice any strong smells near outlets, electrical boxes, or light fixtures, they may be due to an electrical problem. Call an electrician to evaluate and fix the problem. In the mean-time, do not use electrical power in that area.

Removing broken light bulbs
Sometimes, especially on exterior light fixtures, the glass bulb breaks away from the metal base. There is no best way to re-move the base from the fixture, but here are several options.

Before replacing an exterior light, purchase a higher quality bulb with a better base or a copper base that will not rust. You can also coat the threads of exterior bulbs with a special di-electric grease available at automotive stores. Dry lubricant, Permatex Anti-Seize, and Vaseline will also work.

To remove the broken base, first make sure the power is off. Wear eye protection. Protect the immediate area from broken glass that may remain on the base. I like to use a needle nose pliers to grab the metal rim of the bulb and twist it. You can also jam the nose of the pliers into the base of the bulb to get a grip. Sometimes opening the pliers inside the metal threads will give you a grip.

If all fails, use the needle nose pliers to collapse the metal threads until you can remove them.

Folks have phoned my radio show with the following suggestions for removal:
- Use your fingers, protected by heavy gloves (not my idea).
- Use a fuse puller the same way you use a needle nose pliers.
- Jam into the broken base and turn with:
    - a large cork.
    - a wooden ruler.
    - a wad of white bread (perhaps you need some really heavy Italian bread).
    - a potato.

Energy-saving tips for light bulbs
If you have teens or younger children in your home, you may have noticed that they seldom remember to turn lights off. From personal experience, I know that the best way to keep the lights off in a home shared with teenagers is to send them away to college. If that is not practical, here are several aids I have used successfully.

First, reduce the wattage of all lights and replace standard incandescent bulbs with fluorescent lamps. Fluorescent lamps are now available that are small enough to fit inside standard table lamps and fixtures.

A fluorescent costs about 5 to 10 times more than a standard bulb, but it easily pays for itself through energy savings and long life. You will replace the standard light bulb 10 times before the fluorescent fails.

If you're concerned about the color of fluorescent lights, you haven't seen the newer color-corrected types. They produce a color closer to sunlight than typical incandescent bulbs. I have found fluorescents to be my biggest energy saver. They are in all our table lamps and many other fixtures.

For walk-in closets or storage areas, replace the switch with a 15-minute timer. The maximum the light can be on is 15 minutes, and often the kids will switch the timer off because of its annoying ticking. This also works in bathrooms and bedrooms, but there you will need a longer (1- or 2-hour) timer.

For exterior lights, I always use fixtures with a built-in photo-eye control so the light only operates when it is dark. Fluorescent and sodium lights are also big energy savers for outdoor fixtures.

For bathroom and bedrooms, I have had mixed results with motion sensor switches. They can be hard to adjust and may turn off at inappropriate times. Ask yourself: would waving your hands in the dark while taking a shower be fun or frustrating? Despite some problems with adjustment, though, I think motion sensors generally work well.

Chapter 8

ELECTRICAL

Installing and maintaining a GFCI (ground fault circuit interrupter)

You may have heard of a GFCI (ground fault circuit interrupter) or GFI (ground fault interrupter). The GFCI is a valuable safety device that should be installed in bathrooms, kitchens and any other rooms with a sink; in the garage; near pools; and at all exterior outlets.

If your home is fairly new, it already has GFCIs. They have been required in new construction and remodeling for about 15 years. If you are spending the money to remodel a kitchen or bathroom, add GFCI outlets there and at every other spot in your home where damp or wet conditions occur. Hire an electrician to do this job.

The GFCI uses sensitive circuitry to prevent shocks. A tiny imbalance in the power and neutral line will trip the GFCI. The imbalance indicates the possibility of current leakage that could deliver a shock.

GFCI outlets or circuit breakers provide a high level of safety for a very small cost. The GFCI outlet can cost less than $10. In most locations, it can be installed in just a few minutes.

Don't confuse a GFCI with the fuse or circuit breaker in the basement. The fuse or breaker protects the wire from overloading, overheating and burning. A fuse will allow 15 or 20

Ground fault interrupter

the GFI circuitry within the outlet checks constantly for a difference between the current in the black and white wires

if there is a difference (even as little as 5 milliamps), there is a current leak (possibly through your body) and the GFI shuts down the receptacle and other receptacles downstream

note:
if the GFI is in the panel, the entire circuit will be shut down

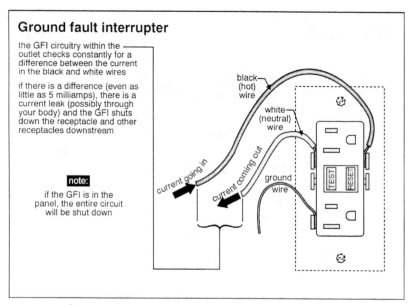

amps to flow through the circuit before it trips - that's more than enough power to electrocute you.

Once the GFCI is installed, test it monthly with the test/reset button on the face of the breaker or outlet. Push the test button, and the GFCI will trip. Reset the GFCI by pressing the reset button. Often a GFCI outlet in one bathroom also protects other bathrooms, the garage, and exterior outlets.

I provide home inspection services, during which I always test the GFCIs, and I've found that about 5% to 10% of the existing GFCI outlets are not working properly.

Doorbell blues

Don't be afraid to try to repair the doorbell. All of its parts are low voltage - 12 to 24 volts - and can't really hurt you. All of the light gauge "doorbell" wire will be low voltage. However, you should not attempt to repair or replace the transformer for the unit. It converts a 110-volt supply to 12 or 24 volts.

ELECTRICAL

Start with the doorbell button. It's the most common source of problems because of its exposure to weather. If the button is recessed or flush with the wood trim, slip a screwdriver or putty knife under the edge and pry it out of its hole. If it is screwed to the frame, remove the screws.

Now you can see the low voltage wires. If they are corroded or are not tightly attached, you have found the problem. Use your metal screwdriver to short between the wires, and the doorbell should ring. You can easily replace the button. If it does not ring, the problem is in the chime or transformer.

Take a peek at the chime. Make sure it is level. Vacuum away any dust. You will see a round plunger that needs to move freely in the magnet surrounding it.

After you have checked these items, the next step would be to use a voltmeter to analyze the transformer and wiring. This is a task you may wish to leave to a professional.

For about $20, you can buy a new battery operated chime and button that needs no wires. The button is mounted any-where within 100 feet of the chime. This is a great option when wires are damaged.

I use a battery operated doorbell to "chime" my son when he is enjoying loud music in his second floor bedroom and can't hear the phone. Some people carry the button in their car to chime the folks inside a home to announce that the car pool has arrived.

Chapter 9

PLUMBING, SINKS, TUBS

Repair a dripping faucet

The newer washerless faucets are relatively easy to repair. Anyone with average "fix-it" abilities can fix a drip or leak. The most difficult part is determining the type and brand of faucet so you can buy the right parts.

Look for a brand name on the handle, spout or base of the faucet. Take a picture if necessary for guidance when you visit the store. If the base of the handle has a circular fitting, you have a ball type faucet. If the handle moves up and down for volume and left and right for temperature, you have a barrel cartridge or disk type faucet. If you are handy and confident, dismantle the faucet and bring the parts to the store.

Now it's off to the plumbing store or hardware store to find replacement parts. If it's a hardware store, choose one that's well-stocked and has skilled staff in the plumbing department. Share with them your brand name, picture and general information on type of faucet. Most repair parts are sold in kits with good instructions.

If you go it alone in the store, you'll need to locate parts based on the brand, type and appearance of the faucet. Most of the repair part packages will have sketches of the faucets and descriptions of parts.

Once you have the appropriate repair kit, read the instructions on how to dismantle and repair the faucet. Some kits also include special equipment you'll need, such as an Allen wrench or spanner wrench. In general, you will be replacing springs, rubber washers and "o" rings.

Follow the simple directions and sketches. It's hard to go wrong. Just remember to turn off the water before you start.

Dripping valves—interior
Sometimes an indoor valve—for example, a basement valve for an outside water connection—develops a slow drip. How can you fix the leak?

Examine the valve and you'll see that the handle is mounted on a round brass stem or shaft. The shaft enters the body of the valve through a hole in a hex nut. If you tighten this hex nut (packing nut), the leak should stop. You only need to tighten this packing nut slightly to stop the drip.

If you overtighten the packing nut, the valve will be hard to operate and you may not be able to turn the handle at all. If the valve is hard to operate, just loosen the nut.

One caution: if the valve has a buildup of corrosion and hard water scale inside, tightening the nut may not solve the problem. You may need to dismantle the valve and replace a packing ring or washer below the nut. To rebuild the valve, you may need to clean the stem and/or replace parts.

Dripping garden hoses
Many of us have problems with garden hoses that leak at the fittings. This is easy to fix with the new products on the market. By paying attention to leaks and spending a few bucks and a few minutes, we can conserve water—a precious resource.

The most common problem is a missing or hardened washer. Open the fitting and look for the washer inside the female end of the fitting. If the washer is hard or damaged, replace it with a new washer.

While you have the fitting open, look at the male end of the fitting. It should have a relatively flat surface to contact the washer. Both of the threaded ends should be relatively round.

If the threaded ends are out of round, or if they're bent or cracked, replace them. You can buy great replacement ends at the hardware store. Cut off the old fitting with a sharp knife and take it to the hardware store to match the inside hose diameter with the new fitting. The best fittings are plastic with small plastic clamps. You slip the fitting into the hose and tighten down the clamp. If you have trouble slipping the hose over the fitting, warm it with hot water.

If there's a break or split in the hose, cut out the bad area and buy a fitting to connect the hose sections.

Dripping water heater
On the side of the water heater is a temperature/pressure valve with a handle. This valve is designed as a safety measure—it will open if the water heater overheats and creates excessive pressure.

When the valve develops a leak, though, water runs down the tube and drips on the floor. A leaky valve should be replaced. The leak can get worse at any time. More seriously, the constant flow of water may corrode or seal shut the valve with hard water scale, and that creates a potential danger. A new valve costs about $20 and take less than 30 minutes to install.

Garbage disposal tips and repair
Some people prefer not to use the garbage disposal in the

kitchen sink, but they "inherited" one anyway when they moved into their current home. If that's true in your case, run the disposal every once in a while to prevent the buildup of any food or waste. If you leave it out of operation, it will eventually freeze up and be ruined.

But let's assume you like to use your garbage disposal, yet one day it stops working. It doesn't even hum anymore. You can perform simple service yourself.

First, turn the unit off at the wall switch. Then look under the sink and locate a small red button on the base of the unit. This is the electrical reset. If the unit is no longer humming, it probably means the overload has been tripped. Push this button in to reset the thermal overload/reset.

Try to switch the unit on. If the unit now hums but will not run, turn it off immediately. You have a jam in the disposal that needs to be cleared.

Check under the sink for a small L-shaped service wrench that looks like an Allen wrench with a bend on each end. The installer of the disposal unit left it there for you (very thoughtful, wouldn't you say?). It may be in a small plastic pouch stapled to the side of the cabinet. At the end of this tool is a hex wrench that fits into a hole you'll find on the bottom of the disposal, in the center. Work the wrench back and forth until the unit moves freely for several revolutions. As you move the wrench, you are moving the shaft of the disposal.

If you can't find the service wrench in your sink cabinet, you can buy one at any hardware store. Or, you can free the disposal by working from above with a socket on the end of a long extension. There will be a hex nut on the shaft inside the disposal.

Now look into the disposal from above. Check for any foreign objects. Remove them with tongs. Run water and start the unit.

Leaking sink mushroom (air gap)

You may not know what it's called, but you've seen it a thousand times: that little chrome "mushroom" on the kitchen sink next the faucet. It's called an air gap, and it prevents the backflow of dirty water into the dishwasher.

When the dishwasher drains, it pumps the dirty water up to this air gap. The water then makes a U-turn and is routed down a drain line. This provides a physical break or "air gap"

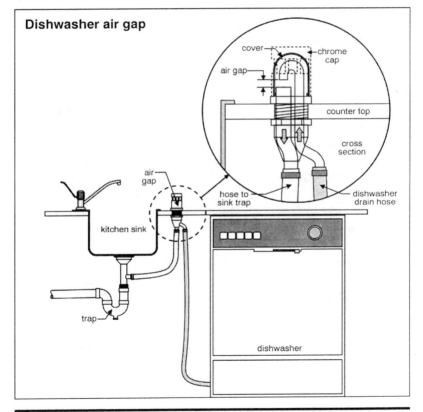

Dishwasher air gap

cover — chrome cap

air gap

counter top

cross section

air gap

hose to sink trap

dishwasher drain hose

kitchen sink

trap

dishwasher

that prevents dirty water from flowing back into the dish-washer.

If the dishwasher were connected directly to the disposal or the drainpipe, a plugged drain could easily force wastewater into the dishwasher. Since the air gap is placed above the sink, any wastewater will now back up into the sink instead.

Sometimes the air gap leaks when the dishwasher drains. This happens if the gap is dirty or there are restrictions in the drain line between the air gap and the sink drain. To fix it, slide off the chrome cover of the air gap and clean the plastic parts. You can often remove the internal plastic cover and clean it, too.

Also, look at the drain line (probably a rubber hose) beneath the air gap. Remove any kinks, and replace the hose if it is damaged.

Leaking toilet tank – So your toilet fills during the night?
It's possible for a toilet to develop a slow leak in the flush valve. This is the flapper or ball valve that lets water flow from the tank into the bowl. A slight leak is normally not noticeable as water slowly flows into the bowl and down the drain.

You may hear the toilet mysteriously fill during the night when the house is quiet. This is caused by a leaking flush valve.

You can test for a leak by putting a little food coloring in the tank. Don't flush the tank. If there's a leak, you will see the colored water trickle into the bowl.

Often you just need to clean or adjust the flush valve. The flapper or ball seats on the top of the pipe leading to the bowl. Wipe the mating surfaces with a rag to remove rust and hard water deposits. Also make sure the valve is aligned over the

PLUMBING, SINKS, TUBS

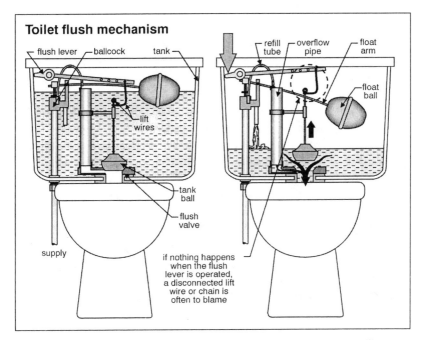

Toilet flush mechanism

flush lever — ballcock   tank —

refill tube — overflow pipe — float arm

float ball

lift wires

tank ball

flush valve

supply

if nothing happens when the flush lever is operated, a disconnected lift wire or chain is often to blame

opening. If the rubber parts are cracked or brittle, you will need to replace the flush valve. Because this leak can waste a large amount of water, fix it as soon as possible.

Re-caulking around the bathtub
If the joint between the tub and the wall has opened up, and water is running into the kitchen below, it's time to think about caulking around the bathtub.

Often, the joint between tub and wall is filled with tile grout or hard caulking that cannot withstand the relative movement between the tub and wall tile. The wall is fixed, while the tub rests on the floor and may move when loaded with water and bather(s).

To repair the joint, first remove all loose material and meticulously clean the area with rubbing alcohol.

Removing caulk used to require softening the caulk with a heat gun, then scraping out the caulk with a stiff, sharp putty knife. If that did not work, you would need to use a hammer and chisel.

But now, 3M has solved the problem with its caulk remover called . . . Caulk Remover. It's the consistency of white glue and even comes in a glue-like container. You apply a thin coat to completely cover the old caulk. After 2 to 7 hours, you'll be able to remove the loosened caulk with a putty knife. If the caulk remains firm, you can remove it with a safety razor.

Thoroughly clean the surface with water and allow it to dry thoroughly. Recaulk the joint with a flexible silicone or urethane base caulk. Special bathtub caulks are also available. These caulks resist water and mildew, and they remain flexible to allow for movement. Be sure to pick a color that matches the grout.

It is also a good idea to fill the tub with water before you replace the caulk. A tub will often move slightly from the weight of water, so you'll be filling the joint when it's forced open, and it will accommodate more movement when the tub is filled in the future. After the caulk has partially cured, drain the water.

Preventing grout stains
It's important to prevent stains from developing in the grout that surrounds ceramic tile. Grout is relatively porous, and once mildew and other stains penetrate deeply, regrouting is the only solution.

To prevent problems, seal the grout with a special silicone based sealer. Sealer is available at hardware or tile stores. Follow the directions on the product. This will keep water and stains from penetrating the grout.

PLUMBING, SINKS, TUBS

Clean a plugged shower head

A shower head can easily become clogged with hard water deposits, reducing a nice steady spray to a errant squirt. Removing these deposits is easy. Soak the head in vinegar or an acid-based hard water stain remover. You don't even have to remove the head.

Place the vinegar or cleaner in a sandwich-sized plastic bag and tape it over the shower head. Allow it to soak until the deposits are dissolved. Remember to follow all necessary precautions for any cleaner or chemical.

Low flow at the faucet or washing machine

A plugged aerator can interfere with water flow at any faucet or other outlet. The aerator, which is screwed to the end of the faucet, strains water while introducing air. If the strainer becomes plugged, the flow is reduced. Remove the strainer and clean it.

The hose fittings between the washing machine and the faucet may contain small screens or strainers. If you have low flow, clean these strainers.

Strainers or aerators can become blocked when water pressure is turned off, causing deposits to collect inside the pipes of your plumbing system. Testing and maintenance of municipal water systems can also cause problems.

Toilet trouble #1: partial flush

If a toilet only provides a partial flush, check a few simple things before calling the plumber. The problem may be with the amount of water or the speed of water flow from the tank to the bowl.

First, check that the water level in the tank is at the water level mark on the side of the tank or near the top of the overflow pipe. If the water level is low, adjust the float by bending its rod or resetting the adjustment screw.

Check for bricks or stones that may have been placed in the tank to save water with each flush. These objects may reduce the water flow to a level that isn't adequate for flushing action.

Pour about 2 or 3 gallons of water from a pail directly into the bowl. If it flushes well, the drain and vent are probably clear.

Check the flapper valve or tank ball that releases water from the tank to the bowl. Watch it in operation to make sure it's opening fully and staying open until all the water is out of the tank. If in doubt, hold the valve open with your hand and watch the flushing action.

Check for a jet flush hole in the front edge of the toilet trap. If there is one, it must be free of deposits. Use an acid cleaner and a stick if necessary to clear the opening.

Some toilets have small holes under the toilet bowl rim that release water to the bowl. If these holes are plugged, clean them with a toothpick. In an old toilet, even if the holes around the rim are clear, the chamber leading to the holes may be blocked.

You can buy an acid cleaner at a plumbing supply store to clean this chamber and the holes. You plug the holes with plumber's putty and then pour the acid into the overflow tube. Allow the acid to sit for a length of time to dissolve deposits. Follow the specific instruction for the product you buy.

Finally, if you're sure there is adequate flow of water from the tank to the bowl, the problem is in the toilet trap or sewer system. You'll need a plunger or an auger (snake) to fix this; or call the plumber.

PLUMBING, SINKS, TUBS

Toilet trouble #2: blockage

An overflowing toilet bowl means facing a really messy job or a plumber's bill. If you're willing to try to fix it before calling for help, here are some tips.

A toilet has a built-in trap that holds water, sealing the toilet from the sewer system. Most toilet bowl blockage occurs in the trap.

To clean a plugged toilet, first bail out enough water to prevent overflowing. Clear any visible blockage by using a toilet plunger. Place the plunger over the large opening in the bottom of the bowl and pump about ten times. Remove the plunger. If water rushes out, the blockage is cleared.

If the plunger fails, try an auger (snake). A closet auger with a bent tube to help feed the snake into the trap is best. Twist the auger as you feed it into the toilet, trying to break through the blockage or hook and remove it. A bent coat hanger will also hook and remove some objects.

If the auger fails too, call a plumber. The plumber will remove the toilet to check for blockage and will snake the major components of the drainage system.

Chemical cleaners are not effective for toilet bowl blockage. Cleaners usually can't reach the blockage, and they complicate any further attempts to remove the blockage. When in doubt, call a professional. You may save money in the long run.

Toilet trouble #3: whistling sounds

Whistling sounds in a plumbing system are usually caused when water flows through a restricted supply line. This can occur at the shut-off valve at the wall below the tank or at the fill valve inside the tank.

First, check that the supply shut-off valve is fully open. Then take off the tank cover. Flush the toilet and listen to each of these valves to try to locate the noise.

You may feel a vibration when you touch the valve. If you can locate the source, work on that valve. Debris, rust, or mineral deposits caught in small passageways would restrict water flow and could cause noise.

If the noise seems to be coming from the shut-off valve, open and close it several times. This may clear debris. Leave the valve open. Flush again. If the whistle remains, you may need to dismantle this valve and look for obstructions.

If you suspect that the noise comes from the fill valve inside the tank, check it for obstructions. First, turn off the water supply at the wall shut-off. In the tank, dismantle the top of the fill valve where the float arm is attached. Clean and re-assemble. Sometimes it's easier to replace the whole valve assembly than it is to repair it.

I'm sure you will find the whistle at one of the valves. If this sounds too confusing, calling a plumber is a good option.

Banging pipes (water hammer)
Why do water pipes bang?

You may hear thumping or banging when water stops filling the toilet tank...or when you turn water off quickly at certain faucets...or after the washing machine draws water.

You may need a plumber to fix this problem, but first you can try a simple trick. Your plumbing system probably has air cushions. These cushions or shock absorber chambers, lo-cated near the laundry, the kitchen, or the main valve, were initially filled with air so that when a valve closed quickly, the

PLUMBING, SINKS, TUBS

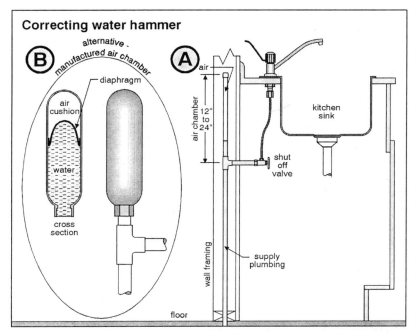

Correcting water hammer

force of the water movement bounced against the air cushion. This prevented the hammering.

Now these air cushions are probably filled with water. To solve the problem, you need to drain your plumbing system. Start by turning off the main water supply. Then open all the faucets in your home. Air will be drawn into the upper faucets. Water will drain from the lower faucets.

When water stops flowing, slowly fill the system by opening the main valve slightly. Walk through your home closing each valve as air is eliminated and a solid stream of water flows through that faucet. After you have closed all the faucets, open the main valve fully.

Now you should have an air cushion in the shock absorber chambers. If this does not do the trick, call a plumber. Re-

member that sediment and air may come out of the faucets
for a short time.

The water-hammer effect can be especially severe with automatic washing machines that have electrically operated water
valves which may close very quickly. If your washer doesn't
have shock absorber chambers, a plumber can install them.
To check whether yours does, look for a 12" tube or 4" chamber extending above the hose bib connections for the water.

Also, check that piping to the washer is properly supported,
because the banging can be compounded when pipes move
around and hit wood framing or other objects. Adding a support may help correct the problem.

Don't ignore the problem. Eventually, water hammer can
cause a break. Have a qualified plumber modify your system.

Preventing water pipe freeze-ups
Let's say your kitchen sink is on an outside wall, and one cold,
windy day the water supply to the sink becomes frozen. You
should be concerned about the situation, because next time
the pipe may break, resulting in a repair bill plus potential water damage.

Start by carefully inspecting the area of the wood framing and
foundation wall near the pipes. Look for holes that allow cold
air to blow in and freeze a pipe.

Check the basement immediately below the sink. Do your inspection on a sunny day, and leave the basement lights off.
Look for sunlight leaking through the basement wall, sill area,
foundation overhangs, and lower edge of the house siding.
Caulk and fill any gaps. Some may need to be filled from the
outside. If this space is insulated, you'll need to remove the
insulation to expose the wood framing for inspection.

PLUMBING, SINKS, TUBS

Next, make sure there is good insulation in the sill area above the foundation wall. Fill the area with tight fitting fiberglass. Pack all areas between the outside framing and the top of the basement wall.

Insulate the supply pipe with a plastic foam-type insulation. You will find this at most building supply centers. Trim the insulation for a tight fit and tape all joints.

If the problem persists, you may need to open kitchen sink cabinet doors during cold weather to allow for air circulation. You could also add a fan or small heater to help move and warm the air in the basement area near the pipes.

As a last resort during very cold weather, let the water run in a trickle at this sink. The water circulation will warm the pipe and prevent freezing. Problem is, this also wastes a natural resource and puts a load on sewage treatment facilities.

Coping with a popping water heater
When the water heater makes popping sounds, the culprit is usually sediment that has built up at the bottom of the tank over the years. When the gas burner is on to reheat the water, sediment interferes with heat transfer between the bottom of the tank and the water. Localized boiling of water within the sediment creates a pounding or popping noise.

You may be able to correct the problem by draining the water heater. Attach a hose to the valve at the bottom of the tank. Run the hose to a floor drain or a pail, and remove several gallons of water.

Repeat this procedure several times over the next few days, allowing material to settle to the bottom of the tank so you can drain it away.

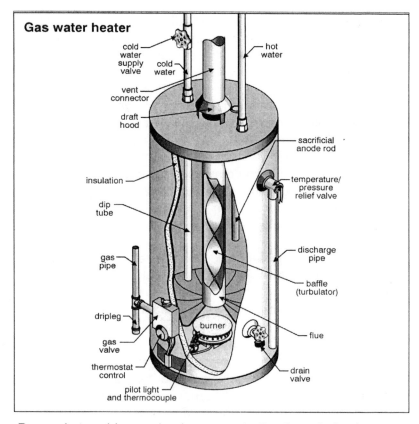

Gas water heater

cold water supply valve
cold water
hot water
vent connector
draft hood
insulation
dip tube
gas pipe
dripleg
gas valve
thermostat control
pilot light and thermocouple
burner
sacrificial anode rod
temperature/ pressure relief valve
discharge pipe
baffle (turbulator)
flue
drain valve

Be ready to add a garden hose cap to the threaded valve-discharge fitting, because sediment often sticks inside the valve and it may not reseal tightly. The garden hose cap must have a soft gasket to seal against the valve.

If sediment has hardened in the tank, you may not be able to drain it off. Eventually you will have to replace the heater. This problem is compounded if your house has hard water from a well and no water softener.

For routine maintenance, remove several gallons of water from the bottom of the tank twice a year. This will extend the life of the heater, reduce energy costs, and help eliminate sediment from the rest of the plumbing system.

Pilot light on a gas water heater

The pilot light on a gas water heater should rarely go out. If yours goes out frequently (during periods of high wind, for example), it may be because of moving air in the flue, but adjustments should eliminate this problem.

To properly light any pilot, follow the specific instructions on the gas appliance. Normally, you first ventilate the area to remove gas residue. Turn the gas valve to the off position for 5 or more minutes. Holding the gas control knob in the "pilot" position, use a match or lighter to ignite the pilot. After the pilot is lit, hold the control knob for about 60 seconds and then slowly release it. Finally, turn the gas control to "on."

Using a long-handled lighter will make it easier to ignite the pilot. Place the lighter next to the pilot before turning the gas control.

You need to hold the control knob in the pilot position for 60 seconds to heat up the thermocouple sensing bulb, a small copper tube located in the pilot flame. When this bulb senses the heat of a flame, a control valve allows gas to flow to the pilot light and the burner. When the thermocouple does not sense a flame, the valve will shut off.

If your pilot light frequently goes out, have the flame and thermocouple checked and adjusted by a professional. Also, ask this professional to check the flue connections, draft diverter and chimney to see if there's a chimney draft problem.

Sump pump clunking

So you're awake on a rainy night listing to the "sump pump clunk"? The clunk occurs when a check valve closes each time the sump pump ends its cycle. The valve checks the water flow, preventing it from draining back down the outlet pipe, refilling the crock, and turning on the sump pump again—over and over.

Some clunking is normal as the valve closes against the head of water. If the noise is excessive, check whether the piping is loose. Pipes that bang against the frame of the house create a louder noise than the original sound of the check valve closing. If the piping is firmly attached to the wood framing of your house, or wedged against the framing, the wood will amplify sounds and vibrations. Hang wire or metal straps along the piping, then place foam insulation between the piping and the straps.

If the outlet pipe is short (making it less likely that water will flow back into the crock), you could remove the check valve. You could also experiment with adding a small hole or vent pipe at the top of the pipe run outside your home. This small hole will allow air into the top of the pipe and break siphoning. The water below the vent will still flow back into the crock.

You could also consider installing a new check valve that may be quieter.

Chapter 10

WALLS, CEILINGS, WINDOWS AND DOORS

Adjusting a sliding patio screen door that sticks

Almost every sliding patio screen door in the world sticks, because few people are aware that they can adjust the rollers that run in the track. You still need to keep the track clean, but adjusting the rollers is the key.

First, though, make sure the aluminum frame is not twisted or bent. Gently straighten any track damage with a file or pliers. If the frame can't be fixed, you'll need to replace the entire door unit.

If the frame is in good shape, the door will be easy to repair. At the base of the door, you'll see a small Phillips head screw in the lower frame. The screw head will be above the frame or in the side of the door, near the bottom. Tightening this screw lowers the rollers; that lifts the door so it rolls on the rollers and doesn't rub on the frame.

Most doors also have a similar roller adjustment for the top rollers. If the door is tight or bound in the frame, you may first need to loosen these top screws to allow room for the rollers at the bottom to be lowered. Don't let your adjustments squeeze the door between its top and bottom frames.

After adjusting the rollers, clean the track with steel wool or a scrubbing pad. Lubricate the rollers and the track with a silicone-type lubricant that will avoid attracting dirt.

If the rollers or roller springs are damaged, remove a sample and try to buy an exact replacement. To replace or inspect the rollers, remove the door from the frame as follows: fully retract both the top and bottom rollers. Lift the door up into the frame. To clear the lower track, you may also need to keep pushing up the lower rollers with your finger or a thin putty knife if the rollers drop down as you lift the door.

If you can't find replacement rollers, you might be able to substitute the top rollers for the bottom ones, since the top rollers don't do much to keep the door on track and they don't wear out.

Replacing the screen in a screen door
To repair the screen in a door, begin by removing the door from the frame. Locate the roller adjustment screws at the top and bottom of the door. Loosen the screws and the rollers, then lift the frame up and away from the lower track. You may have to use a thin putty knife to lift the roller above the track.

Examine the screen material, which is usually gray fiberglass. Measure the door, and plan on buying replacement screen material that's several inches bigger than the opening.

Locate the vinyl spline that holds the screen within a groove in the door. Find the end of the spline and pry it out with a small awl. Pull the rest of the spline out of the groove. If the spline is stiff or cracking, buy new spline material. You will also need to purchase a spline tool to roll the spline back into the groove.

Remove the old screen. Set the door on a flat surface with the groove facing up. Lay the new screen material on top. It

WALLS, CEILINGS, WINDOWS AND DOORS

should overhang the groove by at least 2 inches on each side. Temporarily tape the screen in place.

With the concave roller of your spline tool, roll the screen into the groove. Work on one side of the screen. Lay the spine over the groove and roll it into the frame with the convex roller. You don't need to set the spline to the bottom of the groove at this point. Install the spline around the whole door, working from one end. Cut the spline and force the end into the groove.

Once the screen is secure, force the spline into the bottom of the groove with the spline roller and steady pressure. As you force the spline into the bottom of the groove, the screen will be tightened in the frame. At the corners and ends, force the spline into the groove with a screwdriver.

Now, trim the excess screen material away with a sharp utility knife. Trim over the top of the spline, cutting into the outer edge of the groove.

To return the door to its frame, fit the top section into the frame first. Then fit the lower rollers onto the track. You may need to lift the lower rollers with a putty knife as you do this. Make sure the rollers are adjusted to the correct height. (See the section above if adjustment is needed.)

Adjusting sliding closet doors that stick
Most sliding closet doors have rollers that run in a "J" shaped track at the top. There are also small plastic glides at the base to keep the doors centered.

When these doors become hard to move back and forth, it may be that the flooring was changed (so now the bottom glides rub the floor) or the upper roller bracket is loose. Check the upper roller first. Is the bracket securely attached?

If a loose bracket is not the problem, you can often adjust the bracket and raise the door. There will be a screw and slide or cam that will raise and lower the door. You can see this screw or slide from inside the closet at the rollers. Usually, raising the door solves the problem.

If the floor covering has been changed, you may need to trim the bottom of the door to increase clearance. Remove the lower plastic glides, swing the door toward the room, and lift the rollers out of the track. Carefully trim the door bottom and re-install.

Finding parts for old double-hung windows
Old window parts are difficult to locate. Through the years, there have been many window designs made by many companies. Try one of the following sources. Send them a complete description and a picture of the window mechanism you're looking for:

Wisconsin Window Parts
PO Box 138
Green Lake, WI 54941
phone (414) 294-6229

Blaine Window Hardware
1919 Blaine Drive, RD 4
Hagerstown, MD 21740
phone (301) 797-6500

"Popped" drywall nails
When a nail pops out of drywall, try securing the area around the problem nail with drywall screws. These hold much tighter than nails. There's often no need to remove the offending nail. Simply drive it below the surface with a nail set or small punch. For greater strength, use several screws. Fill the holes with spackling compound, then repaint.

WALLS, CEILINGS, WINDOWS AND DOORS

Secret drywall finishing method

To get a completely professional looking drywall finish, you will need to hire a professional drywall finisher. However, most of us who are handy can do an acceptable job if we finish with a lightly textured surface to hide minor imperfections.

Tape the joints and fill all nail holes with the normal three coats of joint compound. Lightly wet- or dry-sand the surfaces. Then apply a light coat of thinned texture paint. On my last job I thinned texture paint to the maximum recommended (one quart water to three quarts paint) and applied it with a standard thick-napped roller.

The result was a fine texture, almost like a sprayed-on sand finish. This texture covers any slight imperfections and gives a more professional result. You need to apply a finish coat for durability, and a finish color.

Patching cracks in the ceiling

Ceiling cracks are a common problem, especially at the dividing line between the dining room and the living room. This area typically lines up with load-bearing wall through the kitchen and is directly above the beam in the basement.

Such a crack usually results from seasonal expansion and contraction of wood framing. In the attic, the ends of ceiling joists in this area are often supported with a wood wall. The joists move in and out toward the exterior walls; their inboard ends are above the crack. Drywall or plaster at the end of these joists won't expand, and the crack opens up.

Your best bet is a patching compound that remains flexible and can move with the wood framing. Try Krack-Kote, a thick, pliable compound that dries on the surface but stays flexible underneath.

You brush Krack-Kote 2 to 3 inches beyond each side of the ceiling crack, then apply ultra-thin tape material (included in the kit) to bridge the crack. Press the fabric into the Krack-Kote, feathering the edges of the material. After 30 minutes, apply a second coat to hide imperfections. After 30 minutes more, you may paint the area.

The Krack-Kote will expand and contract as your house moves. The material remains flexible and is hard to sand, so make a smooth, flat patch before the material cures.

Chapter 11

BASEMENT, FOUNDATION

Bailing out basement window wells

When basement window wells fill with water, it usually indicates poor surface grading. To correct the problem, the surrounding soil or other surface must be sloped away from the window well. This may require

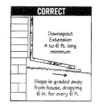

raising the window well. Observe the surface water during a heavy rain, and you will see what needs to be done.

The ground should slope away from the house at a pitch of about 1 vertical inch per linear foot. Hard surfaces such as concrete should slope away ¼ inch per foot. Downspouts and sump pump discharges must be directed well away from the foundation and window wells.

Additionally, the window well should fit tightly to the foundation. The well should extend about one inch above grade and several inches below the window.

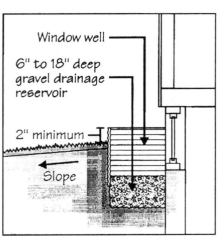

Keep the well free of plant material and other debris. Ideally the window well is dug out to a depth of 18 inches below the window opening and filled with gravel to allow for drainage. Window well covers only divert rainwater; they offer limited protection.

Sump pump basics

The sump pump protects your home from groundwater forcing its way down through the soil into that hole in the ground we call a basement. A drain tile system below the basement floor channels the water into the sump pump crock. Then the sump pump lifts this water to the surface outside or into an underground storm sewer pipe that drains away from your home.

The sump pump and drainage system is separate from the sanitary sewer system that drains waste water from your home to the septic system or to a sanitary sewer treatment plant.

Test your sump pump every few months. Start the pump by adding water to the crock or lifting the float. The pump should start when the water is 8 to 12 inches below the basement floor slab. The water in the crock should be clear, without roots or debris. Watch to be sure the pump removes water from the crock.

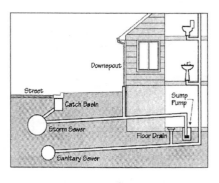

The pump may have a float on the end of a rod or wire. Be sure the float operates easily and can't rub against the crock or the cover. If the float sticks, the pump will not run, and your basement could be flooded.

BASEMENT, FOUNDATION

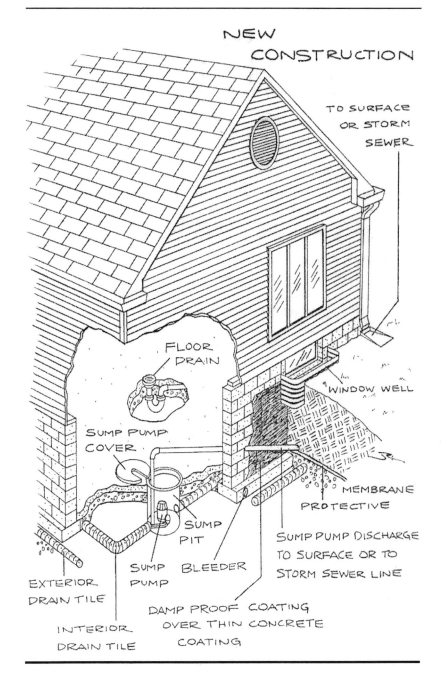

NEW

CONSTRUCTION

TO SURFACE
OR STORM
SEWER

FLOOR
DRAIN

WINDOW WELL

SUMP PUMP
COVER

MEMBRANE
PROTECTIVE

SUMP
PIT

SUMP PUMP DISCHARGE
TO SURFACE OR TO
STORM SEWER LINE

SUMP   BLEEDER
PUMP

EXTERIOR
DRAIN TILE

DAMP PROOF COATING

INTERIOR   OVER THIN CONCRETE
DRAIN TILE   COATING

If the pump is older and worn, rusty, or noisy, it should be replaced. The pump should be securely mounted in the crock. The power supply should be from an outlet, not an extension cord, and the plug should be securely fastened to the outlet.

If the pump runs more than several times per day or runs often during heavy rain, you should have a spare pump or even a second pump mounted in the crock. The second pump could have a float set for a higher water level so that the second pump only runs if the first pump fails. If you live in an area where the electrical power fails during storms, I would consider a battery backup for the pump system.

You might also want to consider installing an alarm that will alert you if the sump pump fails. This could save considerable damage from flooding that could result from this failure. Options range from expensive home alarm systems to a simple battery-operated water alarm. One of the best and most effective for the price is the Water Detector from Zircon Corp. It cost about $12.

The Water Detector is a palm-sized unit operated by a 9-volt battery. When in contact with water, it continuously emits an alarm for up to 72 hours. The unit will float and continue to sound an alarm during a flood.

When roots invade your sump pump crock . . .
If you notice roots in the sump pump crock, they indicate a potentially serious problem that needs further investigation and corrective work. Roots originate in exterior drain tiles, follow bleeders under the footings, then snake through interior drain tile.

If the roots block any part of the drain tile system, they could hamper water drainage. Improperly drained soil and the frost that develops in cold weather can push against the walls, causing horizontal movement and cracking.

Don't panic, but do take steps to investigate the problem. A professional can evaluate the extent of the problem by cutting holes in the basement floor to expose interior drain tile and bleeders. The condition of the bleeders will indicate how severely the exterior drain tile has been affected.

Don't commit to extensive repairs without evaluation of the drain tile system. This testing, which costs about $400, will determine the necessary steps to take.

You should also walk around your property and evaluate trees that may be the source of the problem. A tree's roots usually extend beyond its leaf area (crown). Willow, locust, cotton-wood and Chinese elm trees are particularly troublesome in extending their roots into sewer and drain lines. Their roots can extend four times or more beyond their crown.

If you do use a basement repair contractor, carefully check references. Your contractor should evaluate the problem before proposing any repairs. Contact several contractors. Make sure anyone you hire belongs to the local home builders' or professional home remodelers' group.

Also, consider hiring a basement repair consultant or structural engineer who works independently of any repair contractor. A consultant can help you determine what needs to be done without the conflict of interest involved in selling repair services.

Sealing a concrete basement floor
At times, bare concrete floors generate dust that gets tracked onto other surfaces. Bare concrete also creates a "dust storm" when you sweep the floor. You can easily seal the floor to control this dust.

Now, I'm talking about clear sealer, not paint. Painting a concrete floor is much more difficult than sealing because of the preparation and acid etching involved. Painting concrete can also result in peeling and other problems down the road.

A clear sealer penetrates the concrete, prevents dusting and staining, and makes the surface easy to clean. Look for sealers at building supply stores and cement and brick dealers. UGL and Thoro are two brands. UGL calls its product Clear Masonry Sealer.

To apply the sealer, you must thoroughly clean the concrete, removing all dirt, wax, dust, mildew and loose material. Grease and oil should be removed with detergent. Rinse well with water. Any salt stains (efflorescence) should be removed with an acid etch such as Dryloc Etch.

Apply the sealer per the manufacturer's directions. Usually the surface temperature must be over 40 degrees, and you will apply the material with a roller, brush or spray. One coat is sufficient in most cases. Some slight darkening may take place. Be sure to provide adequate ventilation as you work.

Chapter 12

ODORS

Musty smell from sink
An overflow is cast into a bathroom sink near the rim. If the sink is overfilled, water drains through the overflow hole(s), through a small passageway, and into the trap. Smelly, sludge-like material can build up in the passageway.

You can clean away this sludge. Mix a strong solution of detergent and very hot water. Pour it down the overflow. If the smell persists, try a mixture of laundry bleach and water followed by thorough rinsing with water. If you can see sludge, loosen it with a stiff brush and rinse it away.

Smelly garbage disposal
If your garbage disposal will not freshen up with the normal vinegar, cleaner, or baking soda treatment, the rubber cover may be dirty. Debris can collect under the rubber flaps. This gunk stays damp and creates a strong aroma. To get rid of it, turn off the disposal and use a stiff brush or rag to clean underneath the rubber flaps.

Sewer smell in home
When you detect a sewer smell in your home, there may be a dry trap in the drainage system. Often the smell comes from a floor drain in the basement.

All drains to a sewer system have a "P" shaped trap which is usually filled with water. The trap provides a seal to keep out

Trap terminology

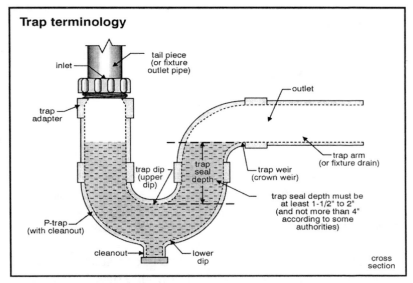

sewer gas. If your basement floor drain is rarely used, water evaporates from the trap over time. Eventually the seal is eliminated, allowing sewer gas (and smell) into your house. The solution is easy: pour water into the drain.

If the smell is noticeable mainly around a sink, try flushing a strong cleaner and bleach down the sink's overflow - the small hole(s) inside the bowl near the rim. When the sink fills to near overflowing, water is routed through an inner chamber to the drain. Debris can collect inside the inner chamber, causing odor.

If neither of these measures solves the problem, there may be a small leak in one of the vent lines of the plumbing system, or a small leak around the base of a toilet or other fixture. You may need the help of a plumber. Check for loose fittings, corrosion, or holes in vent piping. Also, check the top side of horizontal drain pipes. If the top is rusted, it may never leak liquid, but it will leak sewer gas. Drain lines made of copper, steel or cast iron may all exhibit this problem.

ODORS

Sewer smell from toilet
When urine and sewer smells persist near a toilet despite careful cleaning, there could be an air leak at the wax ring of the toilet or in the vent pipe. Rotted or damp wood can also cause the smell.

Check to see if the toilet is tightly sealed to the floor. Grab the bowl of the toilet and try to slide it from side to side. It should resist a few pounds of pressure. If the toilet rocks from side to side, the wax ring has failed.

To replace the wax ring, hire a professional plumber. It's necessary to check the spacing between the pipe flange and the toilet base, and it is difficult to properly secure a toilet in place.

Water supply smells like rotten eggs
Some homeowners have recurring problems with bad odor in the water supply—especially the "rotten egg" smell of sulfur. Water odors are a tough problem to solve, but I suggest you follow up on these ideas.

First, check whether your neighbors are experiencing similar problems. If your water comes from a municipal well, maybe your local water utility can help.

It is relatively common to have this rotten egg odor in *hot* water only. In that case, the water heater's "sacrificial" anode rod is to blame. This rod, made of magnesium, helps protect the tank lining from corrosion; instead, the rod itself corrodes. Unfortunately, as it does, the magnesium gives off electrons that nourish sulfate reducing bacteria. Removing this rod may eliminate the problem.

If your home has its own well, the smell may originate in the well system. There could be sulfate reducing bacteria in the water supply.

To eliminate sulfate reducing bacteria from the water heater, you need to raise the water temperature above 140 degrees for eight hours. Bacteria die out at temperatures above 140 degrees.

To safely follow this procedure, first make sure your water heater has a functioning temperature and pressure relief valve. Also, to prevent accidental scalding, warn users that water will come out of faucets extremely hot and should not be used at the increased temperature.

Finally, check with your municipal water utility. The folks there may have specific suggestions or literature on eliminating problems in well water in your area.

Burning odor from light fixture

If a light fixture gives off a burning smell, disconnect the fixture until you have determined the source of the odor. Overheating electrical wires and devices often emit a burning smell. Don't use the fixture again until it has been repaired by a professional.

A fluorescent fixture may have a ballast that has failed and is spilling tar.

For typical incandescent light fixtures, the burning smell may occur if you're using an oversized bulb. Check the rating of the fixture and the wattage of the bulb. Never exceed the wattage recommended.

You might also have a loose electrical connection at the splice, or a loose screw or lamp base. A loose connection can create excessive resistance to electrical flow, and the resistance causes heat. Excessive heat can make metal connections expand and contract, loosening them further. This heat can damage insulation and even start a fire.

ODORS

You might also have a loose electrical connection at the splice or in the outlet box, or a loose screw or lamp base. A loose connection can create excessive resistance to electrical flow, and the resistance causes heat.

Excessive heat makes metal connections expand and contract, loosening them further. This heat can damage insulation and even start a fire. Sometimes, when such excessive heat melts plastic, the problem area emits a misleading "dead animal" smell.

If you notice any strong smells near outlets, electrical boxes, or light fixtures, they may be due to an electrical problem. Call an electrician to evaluate and fix the problem. In the meantime, do not use electrical power in that area.

Eliminating refrigerator odor

To freshen a smelly refrigerator, scrub the refrigerator with an all-purpose cleaner such as Spic and Span or Soilax. Clean every crack and crevice, and pay particular attention to the rubber gaskets around the door. Remove all drawers and wash all surfaces.

Clean the drain pan located below the refrigerator. You will need to remove the lower panel in the front or rear of the refrigerator to reach this pan. The pan periodically catches moisture as the freezer de-frosts or the refrigerator drains condensation. Most people don't know it exists, and if you've never cleaned yours, you may find some pretty awful stuff growing there.

You also need to clean the drain line from the freezer and refrigerator to the drain pan. You can flush your cleaning solution down the drains located in the bottom of the refrigerator and the freezer.

Finally, you can leave an open container of baking soda, coffee grounds, or activated charcoal in the refrigerator. These materials will help absorb odors. (Activated charcoal is used to filter water in fish tanks.)

Nonsence will also eliminate odors from refrigerators. You can buy it at appliance stores. After use, the product can be refreshed by placing it outside in the sunlight and fresh air.

Eliminating musty smells from wood furnishings
Wood furniture stored in damp, poorly ventilated conditions can develop a musty odor. To eliminate the smell, place the pieces outside in the sun on a dry day. Remove all the drawers, open the doors and let Mother Nature have at it. This will remove any remaining moisture and may improve the smell.

If you can't place the furniture outside, at least put it in a well-ventilated garage or shed and direct a fan to blow air on all the pieces. Allow them to air out for several days.

Scrub the surfaces with solution of 50% laundry bleach and water. Follow up with a scrubbing of 50% isopropyl alcohol and water. If smells remain, scrub with Lestoil. You can also leave small, open containers of Lestoil in the closed cupboard. Placing open containers of kitty litter or activated charcoal (available at aquarium supply stores) in the furniture might also absorb the odor.

If all attempts to remove the smells fail, seal them in by painting or varnishing all interior surfaces, backs of drawers and undersides of all parts. Bin is a great sealer.

Removing smoke smells from home or car
Once cigarette smoke smell has penetrated finish materials in a home or car, it is difficult to remove. Professional cleaner scents used to cover the smell don't always work.

ODORS

One great way to remove or cover smoke smells is with Pine-Sol cleaner. Place several small bowls of Pine-Sol in the problem area and close it off overnight or for several days. Pine-Sol's detergent smell is very strong. Afterward, open the area and ventilate with outdoor air. As fresh air removes the detergent scent, most or all of the smoke odor will be gone, too.

Pet urine odors
Odors from pet urine are hard to eliminate, but these steps may help.

Treat the stain with a product containing liquid enzymes. You can find these products at pet stores. Soak the area with the enzyme, and don't use it with other cleaners. It may take several treatments. Follow the label directions.

Next, scrub the area with a strong detergent like TSP or Mex. Scrub, rinse and scrub several times.

Finally, seal the area with a stain sealer like Kilz or Bin. These provide a white finish and seal in smells.

Don't use ammonia-based cleaners. They can compound the problem and may even attract pets to the spot again.

Chapter 13

SAFETY MEASURES

In case of emergency: things everyone in household should know

It's a great idea for every homeowner to set up a list of "things everybody in the household should know." Your safety plan could involve maintaining a list of emergency shut-offs, information sources, and basic tools. You may need to find an expert to help locate, repair or maintain some of these valves and switches. Locating and tagging them would be a helpful exercise for any homeowner.

I suggest you put a tag on each item and take a tour with all family members explaining what these items do and how to operate the controls. In addition, develop a list of emergency numbers and an escape plan.

So, here is your home-work:

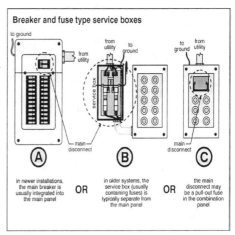

Breaker and fuse type service boxes

- *Main electrical disconnect.* This will be located at the main fuse box or breaker panel. Usually there is one main switch or fuse block, but on older systems there can be multiple disconnects.

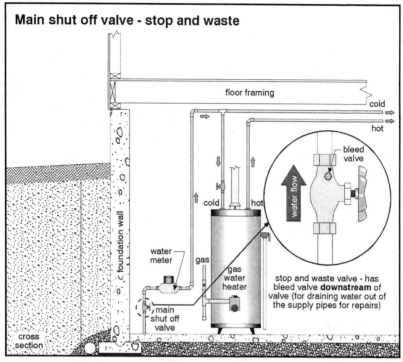

Main shut off valve - stop and waste

floor framing

cold

hot

bleed valve

water flow

cold   hot

water meter

gas

gas water heater

main shut off valve

stop and waste valve - has bleed valve **downstream** of valve (for draining water out of the supply pipes for repairs)

cross section

foundation wall

- *Water main valve.* This valve turns off all the water to your home. If the valve looks old, worn or rusty, have a plumber check it for proper operation. If you use a munici-pal water supply, the valve will be located in the basement on the "street side" of your home near the water meter. If your house has its own well, the valve will be near the pressure tank. In this case, to disable the system, you must turn off the valve and the electrical switch for the well pump.
- *Hot water shut-off.* This valve is located on the cold water inlet at the top of the water heater. It turns off the hot wa-ter supply to your home by closing the cold supply to the water heater.
- *Natural gas main.* This will be located near the meter, ei-ther outside or inside your home. Many of these valves re-

SAFETY MEASURES

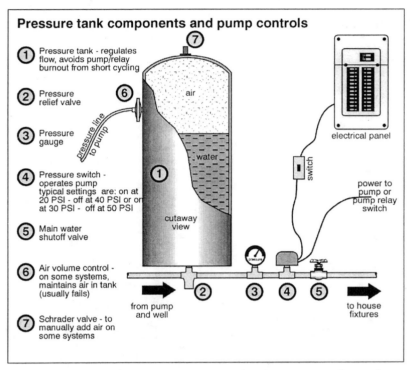

Pressure tank components and pump controls

(1) Pressure tank - regulates flow, avoids pump/relay burnout from short cycling

(2) Pressure relief valve

(3) Pressure gauge

(4) Pressure switch - operates pump typical settings are: on at 20 PSI - off at 40 PSI or on at 30 PSI - off at 50 PSI

(5) Main water shutoff valve

(6) Air volume control - on some systems, maintains air in tank (usually fails)

(7) Schrader valve - to manually add air on some systems

air

water

(1) cutaway view

electrical panel

switch

power to pump or pump relay switch

from pump and well

to house fixtures

quire a wrench to operate; a quarter-turn moves the valve from on to off. When the handle is parallel to the pipe, the valve is open.

- *Local gas valves.* These should be located at each gas appliance; they, too, close with a quarter-turn.
- *Furnace and air conditioning main switch.* This is usually mounted on the furnace. In a modern system, it will look like a light switch. It turns off the central heating and cooling system.
- *Emergency phone numbers.* Keep a list of how to reach the fire department, ambulance/rescue, police, relatives, workplace(s), and others appropriate to your household.
- *Fire extinguishers.* Place fire extinguishers in your kitchen, garage and basement. Make sure everyone knows how to use them.

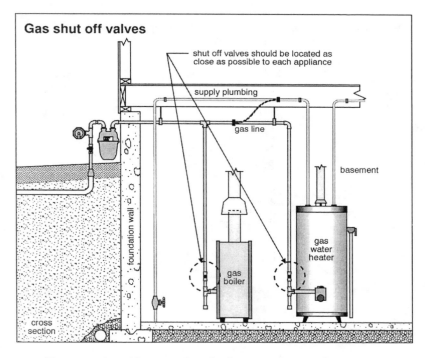

Gas shut off valves

- *Escape plan.* Have a plan for how to get out fast in case of emergency. Establish a specific location where everyone can meet just outside the house. Practice your plan.
- *Emergency release for garage door.* The automatic garage door opener has an emergency release so you can open the door when there is a power failure. Show everyone how it operates. Do this with the door down, because a poorly balanced door may crash to the ground. The release is located where the door attaches to the opener track. Pull the handle to release it—remember, do this the door down—and then lift the door.
- *Emergency release for garage door—with a key (when there is no service door to the garage).* In this situation, to release the garage door opener when the power is out, you must open a special lock and remove a cable. You'll find a circular lock near the top center of the garage door.

Open this lock and pull the attached cable out through the opening. Doing this will release the opener from the garage door so you can open the door manually. Always remember that the door should be down before you test the release.

- *Emergency tool box.* Have a flashlight and basic tools set aside for emergencies. The flashlight should be rechargeable; keep it mounted on its charger.

This is a basic list. For more detailed information, contact your local utilities, police, and fire department. It is very important to know how to react to an emergency and to know that emergency shut-offs will work when needed.

Ensuring safe venting of a clothes dryer

Manufacturers of clothes dryers recommend venting the dryer to the outdoors using a smooth metal vent pipe with minimal bends that can be checked and cleaned periodically. Flexible plastic vent pipes pose the greatest risk because if the bends are not smooth and uniform, lint builds up on the roughened surface. Also, plastic pipe is flammable.

If your dryer vent is made of smooth metal with smooth metal elbows and fittings, you have limited risk. You should vacuum out the vent every year or so through the inlet and discharge. You can use extensions on a shop vacuum. You could also try to blow it out with a shop vacuum. If you don't have the equipment, contact a furnace duct cleaning company.

If your dryer has a flexible plastic vent pipe, remove it and replace with a metal vent and smooth metal elbows and fittings.

Carbon monoxide detectors

You've probably heard about the new carbon monoxide detectors. Are they worth the money? Do they work, and if so, what type should you buy?

I think carbon monoxide detectors are valuable, although they have had some problems with false alarms triggered by quick changes in temperature or pressure, air inversion, or pollution. You should have at least one detector in your home near the sleeping areas.

Your best insurance against a carbon monoxide problem is routine maintenance of gas- or fuel-burning appliances. If you maintain your stove, furnace and water heater, problems should not develop. Also, maintain your fireplace or wood-burning stove and never, never use an unvented combustion device in your home.

When you buy a detector, I suggest one with a digital readout. Place the detector in your home according to manufacturer's instructions. One good place is in a hall near bedrooms, at a height where you will notice the reading every night.

If you frequently check the reading, you can monitor the level of carbon monoxide and react before any alarm sounds. Most of the alarms don't sound until the carbon monoxide reaches 100 parts per million, which is a dangerous level for many people.

If you ever notice headaches, excessive drowsiness, or symptoms of a cold while you're at home and these problems clear up when you're away from home, suspect carbon monoxide. If your whole family feels ill, suspect carbon monoxide. You can't smell or see carbon monoxide, so if you suspect a problem, contact a service contractor immediately.

Radon testing in your home
Radon is a colorless, radioactive, inert gaseous element that can accumulate in lower levels of homes where it can adversely affect human health. Radon has been found to cause lung cancer in humans.

SAFETY MEASURES

Radon can be found all over the country and in any type of building. The EPA and the Surgeon General recommend testing in all homes below the third floor. If a home has a high level of radon, there are simple and relatively low-cost ways to reduce the level.

The Environmental Protection Agency offers helpful publications about radon, including "A Citizen's Guide to Radon" and "Consumer's Guide to Radon Reduction."

You can call the EPA's Indoor Quality Information Clearinghouse at 1-(800)-438-4218 for free copies of these publications. Or visit the EPA's website at http://www.epa.gov/epahome/publications.htm

You can also contact the National Center for Environmental Information at 1-(800)-490-9198 for free information.

Radon levels can vary significantly, depending on the season and how the test was performed. You may also wish to have a professional test done. If you hire a professional, make sure that EPA protocols (procedures) are followed for the testing. A professional test will cost about $100.

Asbestos in your home—what to do
In older homes, asbestos-containing materials were often used for pipe coverings, insulation, heating-duct wraps and even floor tile and plaster. Asbestos can only be identified through professional sampling and laboratory testing.

In many cases, the best way to control exposure to asbestos in the home is to cover or "encapsulate" the material. While removal is best performed by professionals, some homeowners feel confident that they can treat surfaces properly and seal the asbestos with a special sealer.

If you think your home contains asbestos, have it tested by a professional. Also, contact the Environmental Protection Agency and the American Lung Association for the excellent information they provide on asbestos in private residences.

After testing and reviewing the reference materials, you may wish to seal the asbestos-containing materials yourself. Remember to follow all safety precautions to prevent any health risk or site contamination.

Securing slippery throw rugs
Throw rugs placed on hardwood floors can be dangerously slippery. Here are two options for keeping throw rugs in place.

At stores where throw rugs are sold, you can often find a thin, rubbery, bumpy mat that is placed beneath a throw rug. The mat, cut smaller than the rug, stops the sliding. The only problem is that the mat may bunch up or "walk" out from under the throw rug.

We have also had success with Super Grip. When this aerosol is sprayed on the back of the throw rug, it bonds to the fabric and stops it from sliding. Super Grip is non-yellowing, and the rug may be laundered after it's applied.

Chapter 14

MYSTERIES, MISERIES

Restoring Formica countertops
It is impossible to restore the color and eliminate scratches from plastic laminate (brand name: Formica). The same properties that make plastic laminate durable also make it impossible to patch or repair.

However, you can clean and polish laminate with a product like Gel-Gloss. This is a white, milky cleaner/polish much like automotive wax. With a little rubbing, Gel-Gloss will remove most stains and discoloration. After it dries to a light powdery residue, buff with a clean cloth.

This leaves a nice glossy protective finish that tends to mask scratches so that the plastic laminate looks refinished. It also leaves a smooth, sealed surface that resists water spotting and stains. In the future, when the counter gets dull, just apply more.

Never use bleach or abrasive cleaners on plastic laminates. They can damage the surface.

Gray vinyl-flooring stains around a toilet
Gray stains that appear below the surface of a vinyl floor often indicate water damage. When the stains are around the toilet, there is probably a leak at the wax ring that seals the toilet to the plumbing flange.

Try gently pushing the toilet from side to side. It should not move. Once a toilet is loose, you'll probably need to remove the toilet from the floor and replace the wax ring.

You can try a quick fix by tightening the nuts on either side of the toilet at the floor. These nuts, under small plastic caps, tighten the toilet to the plumbing flange. BE VERY CAREFUL not to overtighten or you'll break the toilet base. The toilet is made of porcelain (glass-covered pottery) that will break with uneven pressure or poor support. Turn the nuts slowly, a quarter-turn turn at a time. When the toilet will not move, the nuts are tight enough.

Quieting a squeaky floor

Floor squeaks are caused by loose floorboards and framing members that move and rub against each other as you walk across the floor. The noise comes from wood rubbing on wood or wood rubbing on nails. It's most common in winter when homes dry out during the heating season. As wood dries, it shrinks, and gaps open up. A common 1 by 6 could shrink as much as ¼ inch across its 6-inch width in going from damp summer conditions to dry winter heating conditions.

Luckily, you can work on your floor from the basement below. When the squeaks occur, have someone walk on the offending floor while you listen for squeaks and watch for movement in the basement. Mark the problem areas.

If you can reach the joists and subflooring in the squeaking area, your best fix is to "sister" a 2 by 4 or 2 by 6 to the side of the joist and tight against the sub-floor. "Sister" is a carpentry term meaning that the 2 by 4 is parallel to the joist with the wide, flat surfaces together.

Use a short length—18 to 36 inches—and liberally apply construction adhesive to two adjacent 90-degree sides. Construc-

MYSTERIES, MISERIES

tion adhesive is dispensed from a caulking gun and has a caulk-like consistency. You then attach this board to the joist and the subflooring with several screws or nails driven into the joist at an angle.

The construction adhesive will effectively weld the wood to the joist and the subfloor, preventing movement. The adhesive fills voids and will not release as the wood shrinks and moves. Construction adhesive is the key—it will not shrink as it cures. Use as many short lengths as you need to stop the movement and squeaks.

Although many home improvement books recommend driving small shims between the joists and floorboards, I think this can complicate the problem. How far do you drive the shims into the gap? If you drive them in too far, you can loosen the subfloor.

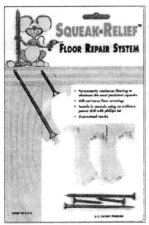

Two products on the market work well to eliminate floor squeaks. Squeak-Relief from Accuset Tool Co., Troy, MI, provides a small aluminum bracket and specially sized screws. The bracket takes the place of the 2 by 4. It effectively secures the floor to the bracket and the joist.

Squeeeek No More from O'Berry Enterprises, Crystal Lake, IL, works from above the squeak through carpeting or hardwood flooring. It is a special bracket that holds and drives a long notched screw. Once driven into the offending area, the screw disappears.

The bracket ensures that the screw is driven to the right depth. Then you use the bracket to break off the head and shank of the screw just below the wood. If you use this on a finished wood floor, it will create a tiny hole that should be patched with wood putty.

Opening the garage door during a power outage

Let's say you've got an automatic garage door opener. It's a great convenience, one you take for granted...until the power goes out. Now what do you do if there is no service to enter the garage?

Your door opener came with a key to unlock the emergency release. You'll find a circular lock near the top center of the garage door. Open this lock and pull the attached cable out through the opening. Doing so will release the opener from the garage door so you can open the door manually.

I suggest you test the emergency release from inside the garage, with the door down, to make sure it works properly. It is very, VERY important to test this with the door down. If the springs are not adjusted properly, a door released in the up position can crash to the ground.

A handle or cable will release the door with a slight pull. The mechanism will re-engage when you move the door or run the opener.

When you test the release, it's also a good idea to have a friend outside the door. If you are confused by the operation, have someone show you how the release operates.

Mildewed walls or ceilings

North-facing rooms may show particular moisture problems. In extreme cases, black mold or mildew grows on corners of outside walls. The framing in these corners consists of several 2 by 4 studs that strengthen the area and provide a nailing surface for interior drywall.

However, there is no room for insulation in these corners, only solid wood framing from inside to outside. Solid wood is a relatively poor insulator. The walls stay cold, and condensation forms. Moisture from the condensation allows mold to grow. You have two options: either reduce the moisture content of the air inside your home or increase the temperature of the wall.

Reducing humidity may be your best bet. If there is condensation on walls, there is probably also condensation on windows that is damaging the window frames.

For the other option—increasing the wall temperature—move furniture or drapes that reduce air flow. Try running a portable fan in the area. Raising the temperature of your furnace or running the furnace fan will also help.

You can also increase the wall temperature by insulating the inside or outside of the wall with a rigid board that covers the edges of the wall studs. This is a major job that requires siding or drywall replacement. If the ceiling is the problem area, increase attic insulation over the cold areas while maintaining an air path for ventilation into the overhangs. Ideally, there should be about 10 to 15 inches of insulation.

If you can't solve the problem through these measures, try an engineer or home inspector who specializes in moisture problems.

Proper repainting over mildewed walls or ceilings requires killing the mildew and using a special paint. See the "Paint and Drywall Finishing" section for details.

Chapter 15

EXTERIOR MAINTENANCE

Sealing pressure-treated wood

You should always seal pressure-treated wood. Do it as soon as the lumber is dry. This wood is treated to resist rot and insects, but it is not resistant to moisture and sun damage. By applying sealer, you can prevent the penetration of moisture and stop cracks, swelling, and splits. By using pigmented stain/sealer, you can also slow the sun damage that would turn the surface gray.

To determine when to apply the sealer or sealer/stain, place a few drops of water on the wood. If the water is quickly absorbed, the wood is dry and ready to be sealed. If the water beads up on the surface, the wood is still too wet to seal. Often, pressure-treated wood is wet because it is processed quickly from the tree to the yard and is stored outside. It may take several dry months for the wood to dry out.

You can also consider using a sealer designed to be applied immediately to damp, newer wood. Select a quality sealer made for pressure-treated wood, and follow the specific instructions.

When sealing, be sure to use a high quality sealer, not a cheap stain. You will need to repeat the treatment every few years. Sealing is a must to prolong the life and appearance of the wood.

Sealing a cedar deck

Before sealing a cedar deck, clean it. Choose a cleaner that matches the brand of finish you plan on using. You can also use Mex, Spic and Span, or Soilax. If there are dark gray mildew stains, add laundry bleach to the solution.

Pressure washing is a good option, but you need to be careful, because cedar is soft and can be damaged by strong spray. I firmly believe you also need to scrub the deck with a stiff brush for a good cleaning. Use a deck brush on the end of a 6-foot pole so your shoulders and legs can boost the scrubbing motion. Rinse well and allow the deck to dry for several days.

I recommend a stain and sealer combination specifically designed for the horizontal surfaces of a deck. Cedar or pressure-treated wood will discolor with age, and a finish with a slight tint can restore a pleasant natural-looking color. A finish with a color tint will also last longer because it more effectively reflects the sun's ultraviolet rays.

You know it is time to refinish a deck when the wood looks worn, dirty, and lackluster. Another way to tell is to place a few drops of water on the finish. If the water beads up, you don't need new finish. If the water flattens out and quickly soaks into the wood, it is time to refinish. You need to refinish every two years if you use a high-quality product.

I don't recommend spraying on a sealer/stain. I believe you need to brush the finish into the pores and cracks of the wood. You can spread the finish with a sprayer, but you still need to brush it in.

Don't use a regular brush. Buy a "rough surface brush." It looks like a thick scrub brush with paint bristles. You attach the brush to a broom handle. Working from a standing posi-

tion, you scrub stain into the
wood. You will find that the rough
surface brush holds a tremen-
dous quantity of finish. You can
apply a uniform coat of finish
very quickly.

Don't apply a thick coat. The finish must soak into the wood. It
should not dry as a thick surface coat that can peel and be
damaged easily.

Cleaning the cracks between deck boards
When you're cleaning or preparing to refinish a wood deck,
you may notice dirt and other debris stuck between the deck
boards. You can easily remove this material with an old hand
saw. You literally saw the dirt out of the groove and increase
the spacing slightly as you saw. This will ruin the handsaw, so
don't use your good one.

Patching rotted wood
Wood rot on windows, doors and frames can be a big problem. If you just paint over the rotten wood, the surface looks
poor and continues to deteriorate. For frames, trim, doors and
windows that are expensive to replace or difficult to match,
patch the wood with epoxy filler.

Several types of fillers are available. I like to compare them to
Bondo, which many of us used for car body repair when we
were kids. Bondo was an epoxy patch for metal that could
make the surface look like new.

For wood repair, you need to remove most of the soft or
"punky" wood. The remaining soft wood can be solidified with
a liquid consolidant. Then you patch the surface with an
epoxy patch. The patching material can be the consistency of

stiff putty or almost a liquid, depending on the type of product and the mix.

All epoxy products consist of a two-part mix. You add hardener to a base product and mix thoroughly. The product cures through a chemical reaction. Setting time depends on the hardener used and the ambient temperature.

You can actually make a wood or cardboard "form" and pour or shape the patch to almost any contour. Once the product is cured, you sand and file it to a precise shape, surface-finish as needed, then stain or paint.

Epoxy is great for repairing wood surfaces. When used properly, it can restore structural integrity.

Cleaning and/or repainting metal siding

Metal siding on a home's exterior eventually fades and discolors. Ultraviolet rays from the sun, airborne pollutants, rain, and other elements take their toll. The finish chalks, fades, and becomes porous, allowing dirt to penetrate the surface. In damp areas, mildew forms, discoloring the siding. Cleaning and/or repainting makes the surface look like new.

You may find that a thorough cleaning is all your siding needs. Clean the siding with detergent and laundry bleach. The detergent washes away dirt, grime and chalking, and the bleach removes dark mildew stains. For detergent, use either siding cleaner available in hardware stores, or a Spic and Span type cleaner. If your siding is mildewed, add bleach to the solution.

My aluminum siding wash formula combines 1 gallon of hot water, 1/3 cup Soilax and 1/2 cup Tide. Scrub the siding with a soft brush or sponge and rinse well. On many parts of the siding, you can use a diluted solution with more water.

EXTERIOR MAINTENANCE

This formula works great on aluminum and will also work well on vinyl siding. Or you can use any easy-to-rinse detergent like Spic and Span, 409, or Fantastic. Just soak the stains with the solution and then scrub with a soft brush or sponge. Rinse well.

To prevent staining, wash from the bottom up. Wet the siding with the hose, and apply cleaning solution liberally with a brush. I like to use a soft automotive brush on a 6-foot pole, applying cleaning solution with the brush from a pail.

You might have to let the detergent solution sit on the siding for a few minutes, but don't let it dry on the siding. Rinse areas as you wash. For larger jobs, apply the detergent with a garden sprayer and then scrub with a soft brush.

In areas with extensive mildew, try Jomax, a concentrated mold and mildew remover. Mix 1 pint of Jomax with 3 pints of laundry bleach and 2 gallons of water. Apply with a garden sprayer per the label instructions. After 5 minutes, rinse off the solution. For heavy stains, scrub lightly. I've tried this, and it works just great.

A few more tips from my recent experience. Jomax eliminates most scrubbing when removing mildew stains. To apply it, I attached a soft brush to a long handle that could be extended to almost 12 feet. Though a little harder to control, it eliminated using a ladder in many areas.

The soft, semicircular brush was designed for washing trucks. It was great and could be used at almost any angle. I also used a soft deck-cleaning brush on a 6-foot handle for much of the scrubbing. Follow all safety precautions for any cleaners you use. Try to avoid working from a roof; it can be slippery, and you could lose your footing.

Cleaning may restore the siding's natural color so that repainting is not necessary. If the surface is dull and faded, you might also apply a coat of Armorall or Penetrol to restore the gloss and color. Test in a small area first.

If repainting is in order, you have already prepared the surface with a good cleaning. Next, prime bare spots and corrosion with a solvent-based exterior primer. On aluminum siding, corrosion appears white and should be removed and primed. Severely chalked surfaces must be primed.

For a top coat, select paint specifically designed for metal siding, or top quality 100% acrylic paint. A quality paint product can last well over 10 years on metal siding.

If the siding on your house is in really bad shape - for instance, if the paint is peeling off - contact the manufacturer of the siding. You may need to check with the original builder or a siding installer to discover the brand and type of siding on your home. Many manufacturers will stand behind their products.

Removing stains from vinyl siding
Unfortunately, petroleum-based products like heating fuel oil can permanently stain vinyl siding. You can't hurt the siding by trying to clean it, but you may dull the sheen with aggressive scrubbing and strong solvents.

According to the Vinyl Siding Institute, for fuel oil stains you can try Fantastic, Lysol, Murphy's Oil Soap or Windex. Scrub the area, allow the cleaner to soak into the surface, and scrub some more. The institute also recommends Soft Scrub.

EXTERIOR MAINTENANCE

If those cleaners fail to remove the stain, try a solvent - mineral sprits, naphtha, or auto tar remover. Use a soft cloth to apply the solvent. Avoid tarnishing the area by using too much pressure. After removing the stain, rinse with water.

Discouraging woodpeckers from pecking cedar siding
Homeowners in rural areas sometimes find that woodpeckers go after their cedar siding—even pecking all the way through to the insulation. Why do they do this, and how can you discourage the habit?

Law in many areas protects woodpeckers. They are great at reducing the bug population. They peck at wood to find bugs, and they bore holes to attract more bug "residents." They also peck loudly to define their territory.

I have heard of two methods that can deter woodpeckers from making swiss cheese of your siding. Try scaring them away with something that moves or makes noise, such as a wind sock, or aluminum pie tins hung from fishing lines. Strips of thin black plastic, 3 inches wide and 3 feet long, may also work.

Distract the woodpecker from the problem area by fastening a block of suet (in a wire basket) to the siding. The woodpeckers love it, and they stop bothering the siding.

Renew rusty wrought iron railings
Wrought iron railings can rust after years of exposure to harsh weather. You must get rid of the rust before repainting. Try a product like Rust-Oleum Rust Reformer.

First, you will need to remove flaking paint and rust, but not all the way down to bare metal. A wire brush or abrasive pad works well, or try a round wire brush attached to a drill. After removing surface rust, clean the surface with detergent and water to remove oil, grease and dirt. Let dry completely. Apply the milky white Reformer with a brush or pad. The product will dry to a black finish in about 15 minutes.

For a finish coat, wait four hours, then apply an oil-based enamel. Some products, including Rust Reformer, suggest applying several coats of reformer for a final flat black finish.

This type of product eliminates the need to remove rust down to bare metal. I also believe an oil-based finish coat will work better than latex on exterior metal.

When exterior varnish peels . . .
Ultraviolet (UV) rays from the sun deteriorate the cellular structure of the wood, turning it gray. This can happen right through clear finishes, and it is the reason exterior varnishes fail. Treatment with a pigmented stain or a UV protection product can solve the problem. Eventually, all untreated wood left in the sun will turn gray.

Broken chimney cap
After years of harsh weather, the mortar around the tile of a chimney top (the mortar wash cap) begins to crack. You should caulk the cracks to keep water out of the masonry and prevent extensive damage from freeze/thaw cycles over the winter. When water is trapped inside masonry, freezing literally breaks the chimney apart.

If the cracks are small, they can be sealed with a silicon or masonry caulk. The best caulk to use is a urethane or one-part epoxy.

Clean the cracks with a brush or air spray and fill the cracks with caulk. The caulk is a temporary fix that's only appropriate if the cracks are small. You should recheck the chimney cap each year.

EXTERIOR MAINTENANCE

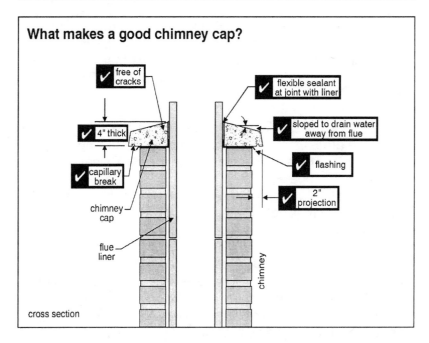

What makes a good chimney cap?

✓ free of cracks

✓ flexible sealant at joint with liner

✓ 4" thick

✓ sloped to drain water away from flue

✓ capillary break

✓ flashing

✓ 2" projection

chimney cap

flue liner

chimney

cross section

A more long-lasting fix is to remove the mortar wash cap and replace it with poured concrete. The concrete cap should be 4 inches thick and reinforced with steel bars and mesh. The edge of the cap should extend at least 2 inches beyond the sides of the brick. Ideally, a small groove will be cast under the edge of the cap to channel water away from the brick.

The concrete mix should be specially formulated to withstand weather extremes and moisture. The cap should have expansion joint material around the chimney flues. After the cap is cured, these joints should be sealed with caulk.
Pre-cast caps are also available in various sizes.
Most major chimney repairs are best left to professional masons or certified chimney sweeps.

Quick patch for rain gutters
For quick repair of small holes in the rain gutters, try gutter

repair or flashing tape. It's available in most hardware stores and is manufactured by several companies. This thick aluminum foil tape uses a mastic type adhesive that's almost like thick tar. The tape comes in short rolls either 2 or 3 inches wide and costs just a few dollars.

To repair the gutter, clean away debris with a wire brush. Wash the area. Once it's dry, apply the tape, rubbing it well into the hole. The aluminum facing on the back side allows you to rub the tape securely onto the gutter. The foil also protects the patch from sunlight. The adhesive of the tape is thick enough to fill small holes and seams. This repair can easily last several years.

Tightening loose rain gutters
Most gutter manufactures provide several methods to hang gutters. During home construction, the quick and cheap method of hanging rain gutters involves nailing them to the fascia board with large spikes. Unfortunately, these large nails often become loose. You can replace them with large screw/nails called Gutter Screws from Fasten Master.

You could also replace the nails with a metal bar or strap hanger suited to a remodeling application. The hanger still fastens to the fascia, but several smaller nails are used. The strap stretches over the gutter, securing the outer edge.

To check the specific installation techniques for your gutters, contact the manufacturer or a local distributor or retail outlet. Another option—one that's appropriate in new construction or when replacing the roof—is to fasten a strap hanger to the roof sheathing under the shingles.

Why roof shingles get black streaks
If your home has light-colored shingles, you may see black streaks on them, especially on the north side. The problem is

EXTERIOR MAINTENANCE

caused by mildew or fungus growth. There is less sunlight on the north side, so the roof stays damp. Mildew loves a damp surface.

The best way to prevent this algae growth is to provide sunlight and natural ventilation to dry the roof. Obviously, this is not always possible. At least keep all tree branches and leaves about 4 feet away from the roof.

Short of replacing the roof, there is no good quick fix. You could try killing the mildew with laundry bleach. Spray or brush a strong bleach solution on the roof and wait until the areas are lighter. Then rinse well. You could also use a mildew wash sold in paint stores for washing painted wood siding.

Several cautions about using bleach: protect yourself, the gutters, and plant materials. Spilled bleach solution can kill grass and bushes. Use eye and skin protection. Do NOT walk on the roof while cleaning. It will be slippery and dangerous. Work from a ladder or use other special equipment. Flush the gutters and metal flashing well to prevent damage. I suggest you hire a professional roofer for the cleaning.

You can also purchase a product called Shingle Shield, which consists of zinc strips that are placed under the shingles near the peak of the roof. The zinc reacts with rainwater to produce a chemical that prevents the growth of fungus and mildew. Again, consult a professional roofer. Although the product inhibits the growth of new algae, it may not remove algae.

If you ever plan to replace the roof or build a new house, keep in mind that several shingle manufacturers offer shingles with a built-in mildew-resistant chemical.

Cleaning dirt and stains from a concrete driveway
The quickest and easiest way to clean a concrete driveway is

with a high pressure water washer. Rent a heavy duty model with a wide sweeping tip, and blast away. You will be amazed at how quickly dirt and grime are removed.

You'll also want to use the washer on your patio furniture, fence, car, and maybe even the house. However, use caution when cleaning wood or aluminum siding. The strong spray may damage wood and caulk, and it can drive water behind the siding.

You can rent a high-capacity unit from any tool rental store for about $60 per day.

The pressure washer will not remove all mildew, rust, oil, or paint stains on the driveway. You must treat them before or after the big blast.

Mildew
If dark stains remain on the concrete after pressure washing, test a small area by dampening the stain with fresh laundry bleach. If the bleach lightens the stain within a few minutes, the stains are mildew and can be removed by bleaching.

If you bleach the surface, use a product called Jomax with a laundry bleach and water solution. Jomax is a mildewcide and detergent that activates the bleach, creating a much more effective cleaning solution. You will need to use eye and skin protection and protect plants in the area. Follow label instructions, and use the cleaning solution within 2 hours after you prepare it. Spray plants in the area with water before and after the application to avoid damage. You can also protect plants by covering them with plastic.

Apply the solution with a garden sprayer or mop it onto the surface. Heavy mildew may require some scrubbing. After 5 minutes, rinse well.

EXTERIOR MAINTENANCE

Oil stains
You can use a commercial cleaner, a strong detergent, or dry Portland cement to remove oil stains from concrete.

Commercial cleaners labeled for use as driveway or cement cleaners are available at most hardware or automotive stores. These are usually solvent-based and require you to scrub the solvent into the oil stain. UGL Dryloc Concrete Cleaner and Degreaser works well. Follow the directions on the product you buy. You may wish to use a product that can be washed off with water.

Most strong detergents will remove oil stains. Try liquid dish-washing detergent, slightly diluted with water. Other detergent cleaners that work well include Spic and Span, Soilax, and Mex. A strong detergent such as TSP can also remove most oil stains if applied with a stiff scrub brush. Scrub the spot several times and rinse well with water. Letting the detergent solution soak in for several hours also aids in stain removal.

Finally, you could try pouring a little dry Portland cement or hydraulic cement on the oil stain. Rub it in with a broom, a brush, or even your shoe and let it stand overnight. The cement will draw the oil out of the concrete. Sweep up the residue and repeat if any stain is still visible. If a stain remains, dampen the powder after sweeping, and the cement will bond with the surface to freshen the appearance.

Cement's fine powder can damage eyes and skin. Take safety precautions. The cleaners described above also use strong chemicals, so follow precautions on the label. Let the cleaners do the work, and try several applications if the stain remains.

Rust stains
Try Whink brand Rust and Iron Stain Remover. You will find it

in hardware and grocery stores. This is a powder that comes in a white container with red
and blue lettering, not the Whink liquid in the
brown bottle. Dampen the stained area with
clean water. Dissolve 1 cup of Whink cleaner
in a plastic pail with 1 gallon of cold water. Apply cleaner to the surface with a soft brush.
Scrub until the stain disappears. Then rinse
thoroughly.

You can also bleach rust stains with oxalic acid
or a cleaner such as Zud that contains oxalic acid. Wet the
stained area and sprinkle with Zud to make a slurry. Cover the
area with plastic to keep it moist. Check and scrub it periodically until the stain is gone.

If the rust stain is persistent, try oxalic acid, a more powerful
oxidizer and stain bleach. It is available in drugstores and
hardware stores and is often sold as wood bleach. Wear protective clothing and eye protection when working with this
strong chemical. Mix the powder in the water and soak the
area with the mixture, then let it stand for several hours,
scrubbing periodically. For stubborn stains, apply more solution and let it stand longer.

Paint
If paint splatters have dried on concrete, a high pressure water washer is your best bet for a first try at removing them. If
the paint proves to be too stubborn, you can still use the
washer to clean many other things outdoors.

Paint stripper will also remove these stains. I prefer a paint
stripper that cleans up with soap and water. Follow the specific instructions for the stripper you purchase, and observe all
safety precautions. Remember to allow time for the chemicals
to soak in and work. You can use a scrub brush and hose to

EXTERIOR MAINTENANCE

clean up after using water-washable stripper.

Sealing concrete
Frigid weather and snow-melting chemicals can easily damage concrete surfaces, allowing moisture to penetrate. The
freeze/thaw cycle of moisture in the concrete creates pressure which makes the surface scale and spall (break into
chips or fragments).

I recommend using a clear sealer on concrete driveways. This
protects the porous surface and keeps stains from penetrating. Sealer also helps prevent salt damage.

Several manufacturers, including DAP, Thoro, Thompsons,
and UGL, produce concrete sealers. These are available at
most hardware and building supply centers. You can spray,
brush, or roll them on after you have thoroughly cleaned your
driveway and allowed it to dry.

Sealing the gap between driveway and garage
Often there's a gap between a concrete driveway and the
garage slab. Filling the gap to keep water out is worth the effort. You can do this with backer rod and filler material.

First, clean the void, blowing away all dust and dirt.
Because of the depth of the opening, you need to support the
filler you'll put into it. Use a caulk backer rod for this. It's a
stiff, closed-cell synthetic material that looks like stiff Styro-
foam insulation in a rope form. Buy a size that is slightly wider
than the opening so friction can hold it in place.

Force the backer rod into the opening with a putty knife until
it's about 1/2 inch below the concrete surface.
The backer rod supports the filler as it cures and allows for
expansion and contraction. It also provides a surface that
does not adhere to the filler. If filler or caulk is attached on

three sides, it can't expand and contract properly, and it will tear away from one side.

Once you've installed the backer rod, add special concrete filler or urethane-type caulk. You may need to visit a cement or concrete supplier to find this product. One type is provided in a sausage-like skin that you squeeze, applying the product like decorative cake frosting. The product will fill the void and is self-leveling. These special fillers/sealers will adhere well to the concrete, expanding and contracting with the movement of the concrete.

Repairing broken concrete surfaces

Small cracks in a concrete driveway or sidewalk are normal and don't need repair. Driveways and sidewalks have control joints set into the surface to limit the extent of cracking, though the joints don't always prevent small cracks.

When concrete sidewalks or steps are badly damaged, there is no easy fix. You can try special cement patching compounds, but most won't stand up to severe weather and will flake off in a short time.

Consider replacing the steps if they are not too large or expensive. Often when concrete steps are damaged or broken, the adjacent sidewalk also needs repair. This makes replacement a good option.

If the steps and walks are in basically good condition, you could patch the concrete with epoxy patching material. Abitron is a leader in epoxy patching for wood and cement. The company offers special products for various applications and provides good instructions.

In general, epoxy will bond well to damaged surfaces and can be cast into a mold to copy an existing shape. First you'll need

EXTERIOR MAINTENANCE

to clean the surface and remove all loose material. Sandblasting or acid etching may be necessary to prepare the concrete surface.

Uneven surface / heaving
If a driveway or sidewalk is heaving and displaced at the cracks, this indicates a problem with moisture and/or the fill underneath the concrete. Try grading the soil to channel surface moisture away from the concrete. The only proper fix for serious heaving is to replace the drive and ensure proper fill and grading upon replacement.

A crack near your home that allows lots of water to leak under the slab or into the basement should be filled with special flexible filler. Visit a concrete supplier and ask for professional-grade filler made of epoxy or polyurethane like that used on sidewalks at shopping malls. This filler comes in a caulk tube that's like an applicator for cake frosting. It's important to use such a filler because it remains flexible as the concrete slabs move due to changes in temperature and moisture. A solid, cement-based filler would re-crack.

In any crack deeper than an inch, the filler will need support from a backer rod—a flexible foam rope that you stuff into the crack. The backer rod is wider than the crack so it will stay in place once it's stuffed in. Above the backer rod, leave space for the filler. This space should be rectangular, and about twice as wide as it is deep.

To make the repair, first clean the crack with water or high-pressure air. Allow to dry. Force the backer rod into the crack, then flow filler material on top of it. The filler will bond well with the concrete. Filler material should only touch two sides of the crack (the backer rod supports the lower edge) so the material can stay flexible, moving without tearing as the slabs expand and contract.

Mudjacking to level exterior concrete

If your landscaping or driveway has a large area of concrete that has settled unevenly, such as a large patio that now pitches toward the house and threatens the basement with leaking rainwater, the area may need mudjacking.

Mudjacking—concrete leveling or concrete raising—is a process utilizing hydraulic pressure to raise and level concrete slabs. A hole about 2 ½ inches in diameter is drilled through the slab. A machine pumps a mixture of water, ground stone and perhaps some Portland cement into the hole. This stiff "mud" mixture lifts the slab.

A proper mudjacking job involves drilling several holes and filling most of the void under the slab. The mud will harden slightly because of the cement, but most of the support is provided by the ground stone.

If the slab is in good condition with few cracks and a sturdy surface, mudjacking is an excellent alternative to replacing the slab. Done properly, the repair will last for several years. The cost is usually a fraction of concrete replacement.

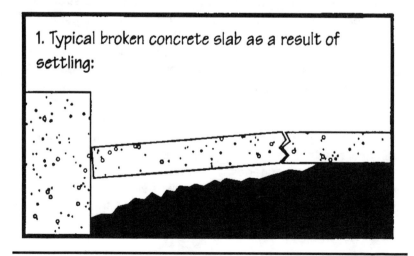

1. Typical broken concrete slab as a result of settling:

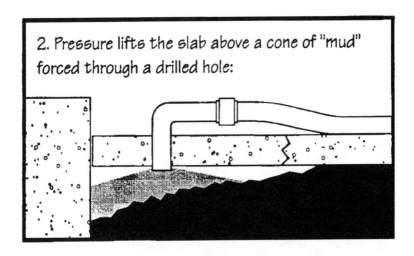

2. Pressure lifts the slab above a cone of "mud" forced through a drilled hole:

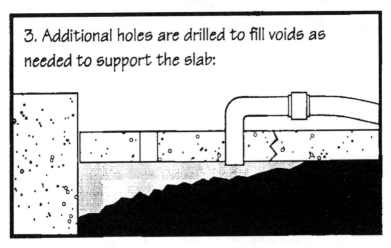

3. Additional holes are drilled to fill voids as needed to support the slab:

Check contractors' references. Find someone who has several years of experience. Check on warranties. A good contractor will provide at least a 1- year warranty. The mudjacking process is somewhat of an art since you can't see where that mud is going under the slab. Problems can reoccur within the first year, and a warranty ensuring free repairs is important.

Appendix 1

RECOMMENDED HOME REPAIR MANUALS

In home repair manuals, I always look for a book with lots of drawings and pictures. I also look for practical advice on day-to-day problems like sticking windows or basic furnace maintenance.

Most people don't need details like how to test electrical heating elements in the water heater or how to repair slate roofs. These jobs are best left to professionals. I recommend the following books. You will find them at any large bookstore.

Complete Do-It-Yourself Manual (Readers Digest). I have an old version of this book, first published in 1973. It was recently revised and updated. It is very accurate, describing all types of basic home repair.

New Complete Guide to Home Repair and Improvement (Better Homes and Gardens Books). This book includes lots of sketches covering almost any problem a homeowner may face.

The Old House Journal Guide to Restoration (a Dutton book published by Penguin Books). If you have a 50- to 200-year-old home, you need this book. It features many photographs and drawings and offers easy-to-follow instructions on maintaining, repairing and restoring older homes.

Appendix 2

IMPORTANT CONTACTS

Air Quality

Allergy and Asthma Network
800-878-4403
www.aanma.org

American Lung Association
800-586-4872
www.lungusa.org

Asthma and Allergy Foundation of America
800-727-8462
www.aafa.org

Asthma Information Center
Journal of the American Medical Association
www.ama-assn.org/special/asthma

Indoor Air Quality Information Clearinghouse
www.epa.gov/iaq

Appliances

Amana Refrigeration
Amana, IA 52204
800-843-0304
www.amana.com

American Whirlpool
800-327-1394
www.americanwhirlpool.com

Association of Home Appliance Manufacturers
20 North Wacker Drive
Chicago, IL 60606
312-984-5822

Black & Decker
6 Armstrong Road
Shelton, CT 06484
800-552-0553

Caloric Corporation
Amana Refrigeration
Amana, IA 52204
319-662-5800

Eureka
800-282-2886

Frigidaire Home Products
6000 Perimeter Drive
Dublin, OH 43017
800-685-6005
800-FRIGIDAIRE
www.frigidaire.com

GE Appliances
Appliance Park
Louisville, KY 40225
800-626-2000

Gibson
6000 Perimeter Drive
Dublin, OH 43017
800-458-1445

Hamilton Beach/Proctor-Silex
800-851-8900
www.hambeach.com

HotPoint Appliances
800-626-2000
www.hotpoint.co.uk

In-Sink-Erator Division
Emerson Electric Co.
4700 21st Street
Racine, WI 53406
800-558-5712

Jenn-Air
3035 Shadeland
Indianapolis, In 46226
317-545-2271
800-536-6247
www.jennair.com

Kelvinator
6000 Perimeter Drive
Dublin, OH 43017
800-323-7773

Kenmore
847-286-2500
www.sears.com

KitchenAid
701 Main Street
St. Joseph, MI 49085
800-253-3977
www.kitchenaid.com

Maytag Corporation
800-688-9000
www.maytag.com

Sanyo Corporation
21351 Lassen Street
Chatsworth, CA 91311
818-998-7322

Sears / Kenmore
Sears Tower
25th Floor Brand Central
Chicago, IL 60684
312-875-1385

IMPORTANT CONTACTS

Sub-Zero Freezer
800-222-7820
www.sub-zerofreezer.com

Tappan
6000 Perimeter Drive
Dublin, OH 43017
800-685-6005

U-Line Corp.
414-354-0300
www.u-line.com

Whirlpool Corporation
2000 M63 North
Benton Harbor, MI 49022
800-253-1301
www.whirlpool.com

White Westinghouse
6000 Perimeter Drive
Dublin, OH 43017
800-245-0600

Associations: Contractor, Supplier, and Builder

American Gas Association
1515 Wilson Boulevard
Arlington, VA 22209
703-841-8667

American Homeowners Association
www.ahahome.com

American Society for Testing & Materials (ASTM)
610-832-9500
www.astm.org

American Society of Home Inspectors
800-743-2744
www.ashi.com

National Association of the Remodeling Industry
1901 N. Moore Street
Suite 808
Arlington, VA 22209
703-276-7600

Plumbing, Heating & Cooling Information Bureau
303 East Wacker Drive
Chicago, IL 60601
312-372-7331

Building Products

Gutter Helmet
888-4-HELMET

Johns Mancille
800-654-3103
www.jci.com

Masonite
800-255-0785
www.masonite.com

Tyvek
800-44-TYVEK

Weyerhaeuser
800-869-3667
www.doors.wy.com

Brick

Brick Institute of America
114490 Commerce Park Drive
Reston, VA 22091
703-620-0010

National Association of Brick Distributors
212 South Henry St.
Alexandria, VA 22314
703-549-0437

Carpet

3M
800-433-3296

Allied Signal
800-441-8185

ANSO
800-441-8185

BASF
800-652-9964

The Carpet & Rug Institute
800-882-8846
www.carpet-rug.com

DuPont
800-4DU-PONT

Host Products
800-558-9439

Monsanto
800-633-3208

Ceiling Fans

Casablanca Fan Co.
761 Corporate Center Dr.,
Pomona, CA 91768
888-227-2178

Emerson Ceiling Fans
8400 Pershall Rd.
Hazelwood, MO 63042
800-237-6511
www.emersonfans.com

Hunter Fan Company
2500 Frisco
Memphis, TN 38114
800-4Hunter
www.hunterfan.com

Cement, Concrete

National Concrete Masonry Association
2302 Horse Pen Road
Herndon, VA 22071-3406
703-713-1900

IMPORTANT CONTACTS

Portland Cement Association
5420 Old Orchard Road
Skokie, IL 60077-4321
708-966-6200

Chimneys

Chimney Safety Institute of America
16021 Industrial Drive, Suite 8
Gaithersburg, MD 20877
301-963-6900
Fax: 301-963-0838

Countertops

DuPont Corian
800-426-7426
www.corian.com

Formica
800-367-6422
www.formica.com

Wilsonart
800-433-3222
www.builderonline.com/
~wilsonart

Electrical

Square D
606-245-7922
www.squared.com

Energy, Energy Conservation

American Gas Association
703-841-8400
www.aga.com

DOW Chemical USA
2020 Willard H. Dos Center
Midland, MI 48674

Energy Efficiency and Renewable Energy Clearinghouse (EREC)
800-363-3732
www.erecbbs.nciinc.com

Gas Research Institute
www.gri.com

Honeywell
800-251-5423

National Appropriate Tech Assistance Service (NATAS)
U.S. Dept. of Energy
P.O. Box 2525
Butte, MT 59702-2525
800-428-2525

Exhaust Fans

Broan
800-558-1711
www.broan.com

NuTone
800-543-8687
www.nutone.com

Fireplaces

Heat-N-Glo Fireplace Products, Inc.
6665 West Highway 13
Savage, MN 55378
800-669-4328
www.heatnglo.com

Heatilator
1915 W. Saunders Street
Mt. Pleasant, IA 52641
800-669-4328
www.heatilator.com

Vermont Castings
Prince Street
Randolph, VT 05060
800-728-3181

Garage Doors

Chamberlain/Lift Master
800-528-9131

Genie Industries
800-OK –GENIE
800-843-4084
www.genielift.com

Overhead
800-543-2269

Sears Craftsman
Contact local store

Stanley
800-447-3853

Government Agencies

Building Research Council
University of Illinois at Urbana – Champaign Small Homes Council
One East Saint Mary's Road
Champaign, IL 61820-6995
800-336-0616

Chemical Referral Center
800-CMA-8200

Environmental Protection Agency
EPA Region 5
230 s. Dearborn Street
Chicago, IL 60604
312-353-2205
312-886-6165

Federal Information Center
414-271-2273

FEMA National Flood Ins.
800-CALL-FLOOD, ext. 180

IMPORTANT CONTACTS

Forest Service USDA
Forest Products Laboratory
One Gifford Pinchot Drive
Madison, WI 53705
608-231-9200

**National Technical
nformation Service (NTIS)**
U.S. Department of Commerce
5285 Port Royal Road
Springfield, VA 22161
703-487-4650

**U.S. Consumer Product
Safety Commission**
Washington, DC 20207
800-638-CPSC

**U.S. Department of Interior
National Park Service**
Preservation Assistance Div.
P.O. Box 37127
Washington, DC 20013-7127
202-343-9573

**U.S. Government Printing
Office (GPO)**
Superintendent of Documents
Washington, DC 20402
202-783-3238

Hardware Specialties

**American Hardware
Manufacturers Association**
847-605-1025
www.ahma.org

Johnson Products, Inc.
P.O. Box 1126
Elkhart, IN 46515
219-293-5664
Kemp and George
800-343-4012

Kwikset Corporation
800-327-5625
www.blackanddecker.com

Larsen Products
800-633-6668
www.larsen products.com

Renovators Supply
Renovators Old Mill
Miller Falls, MA 01349-1097
413-659-2211

Schlage Lock
800-847-1864
www.schlagelock.com

Weiser Lock
800-677-5625
www.weiserlock.com

Heating and Air Conditioning

Air-Conditioning & Refrigeration Institute
703-524-8800

American Standard
800-752-6292
www.us.amstd.com

American Standard Heating and Air Conditioning
800-752-6292
amstd-comfort.com

Bryant
800-468-7253
www.thermacool.com/bryant.htm

Carrier
800-4-CARRIER
www.carrier.com

Heil Heating & Cooling Products
615-359-3511
www.heil-hvac.com/heil

Honeywell Consumer Products
800-468-1502
www.honeywell.com

Jameson
708-963-2850

Lennox
972-497-5000
www.davelennox.com

Magic Chef
800-536-6247

Plumbing Heating Cooling Information Bureau
312-372-7331
www.phcib.org

Research Products
800-545-2219
www.spaceguard.com

Rheem
334-260-1500
www.rheem.com

Robertshaw
800-468-1317

Ruud Air Conditioning
501-646-4311
www.ruudac.com

Tempstar Heating and Cooling Products
800-434-4345
www.tempstarcom/tempstar

IMPORTANT CONTACTS

Therma-Stor
800-533-7533
www.thermador.com

Trane
608-787-3445
www.trane.com

Weil-McLain
219-879-6561
www.weil-mclain.com

York International
717-771-6225
www.york.com

Lighting
GE Lightning
800-626-2000

International Association of Lighting Designers (IALD)
800-423-6587
www.iald.org

Sylvania
GTE Products Corp.
Winchester, KY 40391
800-LIGHTBULB

Marble, Synthetic Marble
Avonite
1945 Highway 304 South
Belen, NM 87002
800-428-6648

Cultured Marble Institute
435 Michigan Ave., Suite 1717
Chicago, IL 60611
312-644-0828

Dupont Co.
Corian Products G51519
Wilmington, DE 19880-0010
800-426-7426

Marble Institute of America
33505 State Street
Farmington, MI 48024

Surrell
Formica Corp.
1504 Sadlier Circle
South Drive
Indianapolis, IN 46239
800-367-6422

Miscellaneous
Eveready
800-323-8177
www.eveready.com

Paints and Sealants

3M Consumer Relations
3M DIY Division
Box 33053
St. Paul, MN 55133
800-842-4946

AKZO Coatings
Box 4240
Troy, MI 48099
800-833-7288

Benajmin Moore & Co.
51 Chestnut Ridge Road
Montvale, NJ 07645
201-573-9600

Bondex
800-225-7522
www.bondex.com

Cabot
800-US-STAIN

Flecto
P.O. Box 12955
Oakland, CA 94604-2955
800-6-FLECTO

Flood Co.
P.O. Box 339
Hudson, OH 44236-0399
800-321-3444

Fuller O'Brien
800-368-2068

Homer Formby's Help Line
800-FORMBYS

Klean-Strip
Box 1879
Memphis, TN 38101
800-235-3546

Krylon
800-4-KRYLON

The McColskey Corp.
7600 State Road
Philadelphia, PA 19136
800-345-4530

Minwax Company Inc.
Box 426
Little Falls, NJ 07424

National Paint & Coatings Assoc.
1500 Rhode Island
Washington, DC 20005

Olympic
800-441-9695

Osmose
800-522-WOOD

IMPORTANT CONTACTS

**Painting & Decorating
Contractors of America**
800-332-7322
www.pdca.com

Parks Corporation
P.O. Box 5
Somerset, MA 02726
800-225-8543

Pittsburg, Olympic, Lucite
800-426-6306

Pittsburgh Paints
800-441-9695

Pratt & Lambert
75 Tonawanda Street
Buffalo, NY 14207
800-289-7728

Savogran
800-225-9872

Sears
800-972-4687

Sherwin Williams
800-336-1110
www.sherwin-williams.com

**Thompsons Help Line
(and Formby)**
800-367-6291

True-Test Supreme
800-922-0061

**UGL – United Gilsonite
Laboratories**
800-272-3235
800-UGL-LABS

Wagner
800-328-8251

Wood Finishers Pride
800-45-PRIDE

Plastic Laminate

Formica Corporation
Sadlier Circle South Drive
Indianapolis, IN 46239
800-367-6422

Nevamar Corp.
8339 Telegraph Road
Odenton, MD 21113
301-551-5000

Pionite Plastics Corp.
P.O. Box 1014
Auburn, ME 04211
207-784-9111

Ralph Wilson Plastics
600 General Bruce Drive
Temple, TX 76503
817-778-2711

Plumbing

American Standard
One Centennial Plaza
Piscataway, NJ 08855-6820
800-821-7700, ext. 4023

**Bemis Manufacturing
Company**
800-558-7651
www.bemismfg.com

Chicago Faucets Co.
2100 S. Nuclear Drive
Des Plaines, Il 60018
847-803-5000
www.chicagofaucets.com

**Crane Plumbing /
 Fiat Products**
1235 Hartrey Avenue
Evanston, IL 60202
708-864-9777

Delta Faucet
800-345-3358
www.deltafaucet.com

Eljer Plumbingware
800-4-ELJER-2
www.eljer.com

Elkay Mfg. Co.
2222 Camden Court
Oak Brook, IL 60521
630-574-8484
www.elkay.com

Franklin Brass
800-421-3375
www.franklinbrass.com

In-Sink-Erator
800-558-5712
www.insinkerator.com

Jacuzzi Whirlpool Bath
100 N. Wiget Lane
Walnut Creek, CA 94596
800-678-6889
www.jacuzzi.com

Kohler Co.
Kohler, WI 53044
800-546-4537
www.kohlerco.com

Moen Faucet
800-553-6636
www.moen.com

Moon Incorporated
377 Woodland Avenue
Elyria, OH 44035
800-321-8809

IMPORTANT CONTACTS

**National Spa &
Pool Institute**
703-838-0083
www.resourcecenter.com

Peerless Products
800-279-9999
www.peerlessproducts.com

Plumbing Heating Cooling
Contractors – National Association
800-533-7694
www.naphcc.org

**Plumbing Heating Cooling
Information Bureau**
312-372-7331
www.phcib.org

Sinkmaster
800-345-8881
www.anaheimmfg.com

Sloan Flushmate
847-671-4300
www.flushmate.com

US Brass
800-US-BRASS
Zoeller Pump
800-928-PUMP
www.zoeller.com

Pumps
Sta-Rite Industries
800-752-0183
www.starite.com

Remodeling
**National Association of the
Remodeling Industry**
800-966-7601
www.ncma.org

Roofing
Alcoa Building Products
P.O. Box 716
Sidney, OH 45365
800-962-6973

**Asphalt Roofing
Manufacturers Assoc.**
P.O. Box 3248
Grand Central Station
New York, NY 10163

**Cedar Shake &
Shingle Bureau**
515 116th Avenue, N.E.
Bellevue, WA 98004
206-453-1323

CertainTeed Corp
P.O. Box 860
Valley Forge, PA 19482
215-347-7000

**GAF Building
Materials Corp.**
1361 Alps Road
Wayne, NJ 07470
201-628-3000

Georgia Pacific
133 Peachtree Street N.W.
P.O. Box 105605
Atlanta, GA 30348
404-521-4000

**Masonite Building Products
Group**
1 South Wacker Drive
Chicago, IL 60606
312-750-0900

**Red Cedar Shingle and
Handsplit Shake Bureau**
515 – 116th Avenue NE
Suite 275
Bellevue, WA 98004

Vande Hey-Raleigh
1565 Bohm Drive
Little Chute, WI 54140
800-236-8453

Safety

**National Lead Information
Center and Clearinghouse**
800-424-5323
www.leadsafetyusa.com

Siding

Alcoa Building Products
P.O. Box 716
Sidney, OH 45365
800-962-6973

**Cedar Shake &
Shingle Bureau**
515 116th Avenue, N.E.
Bellevue, WA 98004
206-453-1323

CertainTeed Corp.
P.O. Box 860
Valley Forge, PA 19482
215-341-7000

**Dryvit Systems, Inc.
One Energy Way**
West Warwick, RI 02893
800-556-7752

**GAFBuilding
Materials Corp.**
1361 Alps Road
Wayne, NJ 07470
201-628-3000

Georgia-Pacific Corp.
P.O. Box 2808
Department M-WDS
Norcross, GA 30091
404-521-4000

IMPORTANT CONTACTS

Louisiana-Pacific Corp.
Marketing Department
111 S.W. Fifth Avenue
Portland, OR 97204
503-221-0800

**Masonite Building
Products Group**
1 South Wacker Drive
Chicago, IL 60606
312-750-0900

Vinyl Siding Institute
888-367-8741
www.vinylsiding.org.

Small Engine
Briggs and Stratton
414-259-5572
www.briggsandstratton.com

Tools
AEG
800-414-6527

Black & Decker
800-54-HOW-TO
www.blackanddecker.com

Bosch
800-301-8255

Cooper Tools
919-781-7200
www.coopertools.com

**Delta International
Machinery**
412-963-2400
www.deltawoodworking.com

DeWalt
800-433-9258
www.dewalt.com

Dirt Devil
800-362-5509
www.dirtdevil.com

Dremel Tools
800-4-DREMEL
www.dremel.com

Hitachi
800-546-5482

Klein Tools
800-553-4676
www.klein-tools.com

Leatherman
800-847-8665

Makita
800-462-5482

Milwaukee Electric Tool
800-729-3878
www.mil-electric-tool.com

Panasonic
800-338-0552

Porter Cable
800-487-8665
www.porter-cable.com

Ridgid
800-4-RIDGID

Ryobi
800-525-2579

Sears-Craftsman
800-377-7414

SK Hand Tool
800-822-5575
www.skhandtool.com

Skil-Bosch
773-286-7330
www.skiltools.com
www.bosch.com

Stanley Works
800-556-6696
www.stanleyworks.com

Vermont American Tool
800-742-3869
www.vermontamerican.com

Vacuums
The Eureka Company
309-823-5366
www.eureka.com

Ventilation
Broan Mfg. Co., Inc.
P.O. Box 140
Hartford, WI 53027
414-673-4340

Home Ventilation Institute
30 West University Drive
Arlington Heights, IL 60004
312-394-0150

Nutone Inc.
Madison & Red Bank Roads
Cincinnati, OH 45227
800-543-8687

Vinyl Flooring
Armstrong World Industries Inc.
P.O. Box 3001
Lancaster, PA 17604
717-396-2377

Armstrong Customer Response Center
800-233-3823

IMPORTANT CONTACTS

Azrock Industries Inc.
P.O. Box 696060
San Antonio, TX 78269
512-558-6400

Congoleum Corp.
3705 Quakerbridge Road
Mercerville, NJ 08619
800-447-2882

Mannington Flooring
P.O. Box 30
Salem, NJ 08079
800-FLOOR-US

Resilient Floor Covering Institute
966 Hungerford Drice
Suite 12-B
Rockville, MD 20850

Tarkett
P.O. Box 264
Parsippany, NJ 07054
800-367-2774

Vinyl Siding Institute
355 Lexington Avenue
New York, NY 10017

Water Heaters
A.O. Smith
800-527-1953
www.aoswpc.whc.net

State Industries
800-626-1981
www.stateind.com

Water Softeners
Bruner Corp.
800-5-Bruner
www.brunercorp.com

Rainsoft Water Treatment Systems
800-860-7638
www.aquion.com

Windows and Doors
Anderson Windows Inc.
P.O. Box 3900
Peoria, IL 61614
800-426-4261
www.andersonwindows.com

Bilco Co.
P.O. Box 1203
New Haven, CT 06505
203-934-6363

Blaine Window Hardware Inc.
1919 Blaine Drive RD 4
Hagerstown, MD 21740
301-797-6500

Crestline
One Wausau Center
P.O. Box 8007
Wausau, WI 54402-8007
800-552-4111

Hopes Landmark Products
P.O. Box 106
Lakewood, NY 14750-0106
716-763-7708

Hurd Millwork
800-223-4875

Lincoln Windows
800-777-0551

Marvin Windows & Doors
P.O. Box 100
Warroad, MN 56763
800-346-5128
www.marvin.com

Morgan Mfg.
P.O. Box 2446
Oshkosh, WI 54903
800-766-1992

Norco Windows, Inc.
P.O. Box 140
Hawkins, WI 54530
715-585-6311

Pella Rollscreen Co.
102 Main Street
Pella, IA 50219
800-524-3700

Pella Windows & Doors
800-84-PELLA

Simpson Door Co.
P.O. Box 210
McCleary, WA 98557
206-495-3291

Stanley Door Systems
800-782-6539
www.stanleywork.com

Velux-America, Inc.
P.O. Box 5001
Greenwood, SC 29648
800-283-2831

**Weather Sheild
Windows and Doors**
One Weather Shield Plaza
Medford, WI 54451
800-477-6808
www.weathersheild.com

IMPORTANT CONTACTS

Wood, Wood Products, and Wood Flooring

Abatron Wood Restoration and Abatron Concrete Restoration
800-445-1754

American Hardboard Assoc.
B520 N. Hicks Road
Palatine, IL 60007
708-934-8800

American Plywood Assoc.
Box 11700
Tacoma, WA 98411

American Wood Preservers Institute
1945 Old Gallows Rd. Ste 550
Vienna, VA 22182
703-893-4005
www.awpi.org

Bruce Hardwood Floors
16803 Dallas Parkway
Dallas, TX 75248
800-722-4647

Cabot Stains
800-877-8246

California Redwood Association
888-225-7339
www.calredwood.org

DAP Inc.
Box 277
Dayton, OH 45401-0277

Hardwood Council
412-281-4980
www.hardwoodcouncil.com

Hardwood Manufacturers Association
400 Penn Cent. Blvd. Ste 530
Pittsburgh, PA 15235
412-829-0770

Hardwood Plywood & Veneer Association
703-435-2000
www.hpva.org

Harris Tarkett
P.O. Box 300
Johnson City, TN 37605
615-928-3122

Hartco Wood Flooring
900 S. Gay Street
Knoxville, TN 37902

**Maple Flooring
Manufacturers Association**
847-480-9138
www.maplefloor.com

**Minwax Wood Hardener
Minwax High Performance
Wood Filler**
800-462-0194

**Mr. Mac's Wood Fix
Mr. Mac's Concrete Fix**
800-348-3571

**National Oak Flooring
Manufacturers Association**
901-526-5016
www.nofma.org

Norton Company
Consumer Products Div.
One New Bond Street
Worcester, MA 01606

Oak Flooring Institute
P.O. Box 3009
Memphis, TN 383173-0009
901-562-5016

**Southern Forest Products
Association**
504-443-4464
ww.southernpine.com

**Southern Pine Marketing
Council**
P.O. Box 52468
New Orleans, LA 70152
504-443-4464

**Western Wood Products
Association**
Yeon Building
522 S.W. Fifth Avenue
Portland, OR 97204-2122
503-224-3930
www.wwpa.org

Weyerhaeuser
800-548-5767

Wolman-Loppers
800-556-7737

INDEX

air conditioner
    adjusting air returns, 49
    noise at start-up, 54
    seasonal shutdown/restart, 56
    tons of capacity, 57
    whether to cover, 55
asbestos treatment or removal, 121
basement
    heating rec room, 61
    reducing dampness, 60
    roots in sump pump crock, 104
    sump pump basics, 102
    window wells, 101
basement floor, sealing, 105
bathtub
    caulking, 83
    cleaning, 36
brass fireplace, cleaning, 44
broken light bulb, 70
cabinets
    refinishing, 22
    removing stains, 40

repainting, 14
carbon monoxide detectors, 119
caulk
    baththub, 83
    use when painting, 7
cedar deck, sealing, 130
chimney cap, 136
concrete
    cleaning, 139
    mildew, 140
    oil stains, 140
    paint stains, 142
    patching, 144
    rust stains, 141
    sealing basement floor, 105
    sealing exterior, 142
    sealing gap by garage, 143
condensation on windows, 59
countertops, Formica, restoring, 40, 123
crayon marks on walls, 11
dampness
    in basement, 60
    throughout house, 59

deck
    cleaning between cracks,
        131
    sealing, 82130
doorbell repair, 74
drywall
    finishing, 99
    popping nails, 11, 98
    repair with spackling, 10
faucet
    low flow, 85
    repair and replacement, 77
fireplace
    cleaning metal, 44
    cleaning smoke stains, 44
    restoring sandstone by
        painting, 16
fireplace glass, cleaning, 34
floors
    quieting squeaks, 124
    stains on vinyl, 123
fluorescent light
    burning smell, 69
    buzzing, 69
Formica, restoring, 40, 123
frozen water pipes, 90
furnace
    "no heat" problem in winter,
        49
    adjusting air returns, 49
    changing filter, 51
    high-efficiency gas, 48
    noise at start-up, 54
    operation, 47
    service requirements, 53
garage door opener, 118, 126

garbage disposal, 79
garbage disposal odor, 107
gas stovetop burners, 66
ground fault circuit interrupter,
    73
grout, cleaning and sealing,
    38, 83
heating and cooling
    "no heat" problem in winter,
        49
    adjusting air returns, 49
    basement rec room, 61
    rerouting drain hose, 58
humidifiers, 62
kitchen sink
    leak in air gap, 82
light bulbs
    burning odor, 69, 110
    buzzing, 69
    energy-saving tips, 71
    removing broken bulbs, 70
marble, removing stains, 42
masking tape removal, 43
mildew
    on exterior, 13
    on walls or ceilings, 12, 126
moisture
    in basement, 60
    throughout house, 59
mudjacking, 145
nails in drywall, 11, 98
odors
    burning smell in light fixture,
        110
    cigarette smell, 112
    garbage disposal, 107

INDEX

in refrigerator, 111
in wood furniture, 112
pets, 113
rotten egg smell in water, 109
sewer smell from toilet, 109
sewer smell in home, 107
opener, garage door, 118, 126
paint
  brushes, 8
  caulking joints, 7
  covering crayon marks, 11
  covering stains, 13
  dishwasher touch-ups, 67
  interior metal finishes, 67
  mildewed areas, 12
  over varnished cabinets, 22
  paneling, 17
  peeling, in bathroom, 12
  preparation (masking), 6
  priming surface, 4
  removing dried splatters, 14
  repainting kitchen cabinets, 14
  selection, 5
  stripping, 27
  surface preparation, 3
  surfaces of appliances, 67
  tools, 7
paneling
  painting over, 17
patio door, un-sticking, 95
patio, leveling by mudjacking, 145
pilot light
  on furnace, 54

on gas stove, 66
on water heater, 93
plumbing noises
  banging water pipes (water hammer), 88
  popping water heater, 91
  sump pump clunking, 93
  whistling sounds in toilet, 87
porcelain fixtures, cleaning, 39
pressure-treated wood, sealing, 129
rain gutters
  quick patch, 137
refinishing wood furniture, 26
refrigerator
  cleaning coils, 65
  odor, 111
  restarting after moving, 66
roof shingles, cleaning, 138
rust
  on bathtub, 36
  on wrought iron, 135
scratches
  in woodwork, 23
screen door replacement, 96
sealing
  cedar deck, 130
  pressure-treated wood, 129
  wood deck, 130
sewer smell
  from toilet, 109
  in home, 107
shelf paper removal, 43
shingles, cleaning, 138
shower door, cleaning, 34, 36
shower head, cleaning, 85

siding, exterior
  cleaning, 132
  discouraging woodpeckers, 135
  repainting, 132
  stain removal from vinyl, 134
sink, kitchen
  leak in air gap, 81
smoke smells, removing, 112
soap scum in bathtub, 36
spackling compound, 10
stain removal, 33
staining
  steel door, 18
stains
  on bathtub, 36
  on cabinet doors, 40
  on concrete, 139
  on marble, 42
  on shower door, 37
  on vinyl siding, 134
  white rings on wood, 42
stovetop burners, 66
sump pump
  clunking, 93
  operation, 102
  roots in crock, 104
toilet problems
  blockage, 87
  partial flush, 85
  tank leak, 82
valve, dripping, 78
varnish
  exterior, peeling, 136
  preventing bubbles & "craters" in, 24

vinyl flooring stains, 123
wallpaper
  removing, 19
  seam repair, 20
walls
  repairing cracks, 4
water
  low flow, 85
  rotten egg smell in, 109
water heater
  dripping, 79
  pilot light, 93
  popping, 91
water pipes, frozen, 90
window wells in basement, 101
windows
  finding replacement parts, 98
  washing, 34
wood deck, sealing, 130
wood filler / putty, 21
wood finishes
  refinishing, 26
  removing stains, 40
wood flooring
  removing stains, 26
woodwork
  fixing scratches, 23
  patching rotted areas, 131
  removing stains, 41
wrought iron railings, 135

SEMINARS AND KEYNOTES

Mr. Fix-It is available for seminars and keynote presentations. Mixing his more than 25 years of engineering experience with "hands-on" home repair expertise, Tom delivers informative and humorous presentations that are perfect for home shows, spouse programs, dinner meetings, seminars, and retail events.

Here's a sampling of Tom's presentations.

Keynote
So You Cut It Twice and It's Still Too Short?
An upbeat look at home repairs. Tom relies on years of experience to relate great stories, humor, and tips with an emphasis on success.

Seminar
Just Fix It: The Absolute Best Repair Products
Tom solves the most common fix-it problems using state-of-the-art tools and techniques. Learn to achieve results you never dreamed possible. Enjoy product samples and hot repair tips you can use instantly.

Seminar
Painting Pointers
Toss that roller tray and forget the ladder. Achieve professional results using the proper tools and techniques. Make interior and exterior finishes look and last as if painted by a professional.

For more information, contact:

Tom Feiza, Mr. Fix-It, Inc.
P.O. Box 510724
New Berlin WI 53151

Phone: 262/786-7878
Fax: 262/786-7877

E-mail: Tom@misterfix-it.com
Web site: *www.misterfix-it.com*

MORE GREAT SOURCES OF HOME INFORMATION

Special thanks to Alan Carson, who supplied 15 great drawings for this book. Alan and his firm, Carson Dunlop & Associates, provide home inspection services and excellent training, training materials, report forms and study courses for the home inspection industry. You can contact him at:

Carson Dunlop & Associates Limited
120 Carlton Street, Suite 407
Toronto, Ontario Canada
M5A 4K2
Phone: 800/268-7070
Fax: 416/964-0683
Web site: *www.carsondunlop.com*

Special thanks also to John Krigger, who supplied three excellent drawings for this book. John provides training and writes outstanding books on residential energy conservation, home cooling, and mobile homes. His book *Your Mobile Home* is perhaps the only book available on mobile home repair and energy conservation. You can contact him at:

Saturn Resource Management
324 Fuller Avenue, N-13
Helena MT 59601
Phone: 800/735-0577
Fax: 406/442-1316
Web site: *www.residential-energy.com*

ORDERING INFORMATION

Copies of this book, *Just Fix It*, are available through book retailers or from Tom Feiza—Mr. Fix-It, Inc.

To order books from Mr. Fix-It, send $14.95 apiece plus $3.00 shipping and handling for the first book and $1.00 for each additional book. Wisconsin residents must add 5% for sales tax.

Send your order with complete return address to:

Tom Feiza, Mr. Fix-It Inc.
P.O. Box 510724
New Berlin WI 53151

SPECIAL OFFER!
Tom's new book *How To Operate Your Home* will be available in late 1999. This operating manual for your home is like the operating manual that comes with a new car. Learning how to operate your home can improve your habitat, save thousands in repair costs, and prevent potential disasters. Advance copies are available at a discounted price of $15.95 plus shipping and handling.

You can also contact Tom and find great home repair information at his web site: *www.misterfix-it.com*